Japanese Popular Culture and Contents Tourism

Contents tourism is tourism induced by the contents (narratives, characters, locations and other creative elements) of films, novels, games, manga, anime, television dramas and other forms of popular culture. Amidst the boom in global interest in Japanese popular culture, the utilization of popular culture to induce tourism domestically and internationally has been central to the "Cool Japan" strategy and, since 2005, government policy for local community revitalization. This book presents four main case studies of contents tourism: the phenomenon of "anime pilgrimage" to sites appearing in animated film; the travel behaviours and "pop-spiritualism" of female history fans to heritage sites; the collaboration between local community, fans and copyright holders that underpinned an anime-induced tourism boom in a small town north of Tokyo; and the large-scale economic impacts of tourism induced by NHK's annual samurai period drama (Taiga Drama). It is the first major collection of articles published in English about media-induced tourism in Japan using the "contents tourism" approach. This book will be of particular interest to students and researchers of media and tourism studies in Asia.

This book was previously published as a special issue of *Japan Forum*.

Philip Seaton is a Professor in the Research Faculty of Media and Communication, Hokkaido University, Japan, where he is the convenor of the Modern Japanese Studies Program. He is the author of *Japan's Contested War Memories* (Routledge, 2007), *Voices from the Shifting Russo-Japanese Border* (Routledge, 2015, co-edited with Svetlana Paichadze) and numerous articles on war and memory in Japan.

Takayoshi Yamamura is a Professor in the Center for Advanced Tourism Studies, Hokkaido University, Japan. His main research interests are cultural tourism planning and media design, cultural resource management and heritage tourism studies. He is the author of *Community Development through Anime and Manga* (*Anime, manga de chiiki shinkō*, Tokoyo Hōrei Shuppan) and numerous other articles on heritage and pop culture tourism.

Japanese Popular Culture and Contents Tourism

Edited by
Philip Seaton and Takayoshi Yamamura

Routledge
Taylor & Francis Group

LONDON AND NEW YORK

First published 2014 by Routledge

2 Park Square, Milton Park, Abingdon, Oxfordshire OX14 4RN
711 Third Avenue, New York, NY 10017

Routledge is an imprint of the Taylor & Francis Group, an informa business

First issued in paperback 2018

British Library Cataloguing in Publication Data
A catalogue record for this book is available from the British Library

ISBN 13: 978-1-138-69408-8 (hbk)
ISBN 13: 978-0-367-02940-1 (pbk)

Typeset in Plantin
by RefineCatch Limited, Bungay, Suffolk

Publisher's Note
The publisher accepts responsibility for any inconsistencies that may have
arisen during the conversion of this book from journal articles to book chapters,
namely the possible inclusion of journal terminology.

Disclaimer
Every effort has been made to contact copyright holders for their permission to
reprint material in this book. The publishers would be grateful to hear from any
copyright holder who is not here acknowledged and will undertake to rectify
any errors or omissions in future editions of this book.

Contents

Citation Information

The chapters in this book were originally published in *Japan Forum*, volume 27, issue 1 (March 2015). When citing this material, please use the original page numbering for each article, as follows:

Chapter 1
Japanese Popular Culture and Contents Tourism – Introduction
Philip Seaton and Takayoshi Yamamura
Japan Forum, volume 27, issue 1 (March 2015) pp. 1–11

Chapter 2
Otaku tourism and the anime pilgrimage phenomenon in Japan
Takeshi Okamoto
Japan Forum, volume 27, issue 1 (March 2015) pp. 12–36

Chapter 3
Rekijo, *pilgrimage and 'pop-spiritualism': pop-culture-induced heritage tourism of/for young women*
Akiko Sugawa-Shimada
Japan Forum, volume 27, issue 1 (March 2015) pp. 37–58

Chapter 4
Contents tourism and local community response: Lucky star *and collaborative anime-induced tourism in Washimiya*
Takayoshi Yamamura
Japan Forum, volume 27, issue 1 (March 2015) pp. 59–81

Chapter 5
Taiga dramas and tourism: historical contents as sustainable tourist resources
Philip Seaton
Japan Forum, volume 27, issue 1 (March 2015) pp. 82–103

For any permission-related enquiries please visit:
http://www.tandfonline.com/page/help/permissions

Japanese Popular Culture and Contents Tourism – Introduction

PHILIP SEATON AND TAKAYOSHI YAMAMURA

Abstract: This introduction to the special issue on 'Japanese Popular Culture and Contents Tourism' places the four articles in theoretical and contextual perspective. Contents tourism is a theoretical concept that originated in Japan. Its closest counterpart in the English-language literature at present is film-induced tourism or media-induced tourism. Contents tourism is placed within the theoretical context of cultural tourism and the rationale for its focus on narratives, characters and other creative elements over media format (for example, cinema) is explained. The article then gives a brief chronological overview of how contents tourism has worked its way into the official language of government economic and tourism policy up to and including 2013.

This special edition brings together four articles on the topic of Japanese popular culture and contents tourism. Worldwide there is growing interest in the ways that films, novels, comics, games and other forms of popular culture act as tourism drivers, for example, when fans go to the locations of favourite television dramas, take studio tours in Hollywood, visit museums in the hometowns of famous authors or have their picture taken with Mickey Mouse at Disneyland. This special edition not only brings together some important case studies from Japan, but also highlights the theoretical contributions that those Japanese case studies and the Japanese scholarly literature on contents tourism have made.

In the English-language literature, the study of tourism induced by popular culture has often been broken down by media format, so there is film-induced tourism, TV tourism, literature tourism and so on (Beeton, Yamamura and Seaton 2013, p. 142). The field is also relatively young. The first major example of a film significantly affecting tourist behaviour is believed to have been the

1935 film *The mutiny on the Bounty*, which sparked an influx of tourists to Tahiti (Roesch 2009, p. 9). But it was not until 1996 that the then British Tourism Association 'was the first tourism organization that tried to capitalize on film tourism through the publication of a movie map featuring locations from various films shot in Great Britain' (ibid., p. 3). Beeton's *Film-induced tourism* (2005) is broadly acknowledged as the 'first definitive work about film-induced tourism',[1] and her book was notable not only for bringing together the variety of different themes within the field hitherto presented in many separate papers and case studies, but also for expanding the previous focus on movie-induced tourism (mainly Hollywood movies) 'to include television, video and DVD' (Beeton 2005, p. 9).

Within Japan, however, the buzzword in the Japanese academy, and the term adopted by the Japanese government in its official promotional strategies regarding film-induced tourism, is *kontentsu tsūrizumu* (contents tourism).[2] Contents tourism focuses not on the media format but primarily on the contents, namely the narratives, characters and locations. This concept is of particular use in an age of 'multi-use' or the 'media mix' (Yamamura 2011, p. 50), when the same characters and narratives may be sold as novels, films, games, toys and cartoons simultaneously, with sequels and prequels added to expand the franchise even further. Steinberg (2012, p. viii) identifies incidences of the media mix, also known as convergence in the English-language literature, back to the 1960s in the context of the anime media mix generated by *Astro boy*. For Yamamura, however, multi-use and the media mix really took off in the 1990s. He identifies three key periods: the 1990s, when multi-use between manga, anime and games mushroomed; the early 2000s, when the internet made digital production and sharing of contents accessible to the masses; and from the 2000s onwards when local communities can be thought of as 'media' because they became increasingly involved in the production and marketing of contents, and their spaces are increasingly mediatized (via museums, monuments and websites). This third stage, when geographical place and contents get linked together in a commercial partnership, is when the economic potential for contents tourism really emerges.

However, just as examples of the media mix can be found, with hindsight, considerably further back into history than the existence of the term that has come to describe the contemporary phenomenon, so too has contents tourism come to be seen as a new term that describes essentially a very old phenomenon. Masubuchi (2010, p. 29), for example, has argued that the visits by Japanese people in the Edo period to places made famous by the poetry of Bashō Matsuo may be considered an early form of contents tourism. Furthermore, as the articles in this special edition indicate (particularly those by Akiko Sugawa-Shimada and Philip Seaton), contents tourism in Japan has had a vibrant history since at least the 1970s.

In the remainder of this short introduction, we place contents tourism within the broader context of tourism studies and highlight the Japanese government policy context before describing the particular contributions of the four articles to this emerging field of scholarship.

Film-induced tourism and/or contents tourism

Film-induced tourism and contents tourism are forms of cultural tourism, which is 'an umbrella term for a wide range of related activities, including historical tourism, ethnic tourism, arts tourism, museum tourism, and others' (McKercher and du Cros 2009, p. 6). McKercher and du Cros present a typology of cultural tourists according to motivation (the importance of cultural tourism in the decision to visit a destination) and experience sought (from deep to shallow). This provides a useful framework within which to see the complex variations within the categories of film-induced and contents tourism. It is shown in Table 1 along with representative examples from the film-induced tourism literature.

As Table 1 indicates, cultural tourism encompasses a wide range of touristic experiences, which makes it very hard to generalize about the motivations and experiences of film tourists. As the articles in this series will demonstrate, the behaviours of contents tourists in Japan are equally complex. Some are fans who have repeatedly visited a community where their favourite anime was set, almost

Table 1 Cultural tourist typology and its relation to film-induced tourism. Columns 1–3 adapted from McKercher and du Cros (2009, pp. 140, 144). Column 4 completed using ideas and examples from Beeton (2005) and Roesch (2009).

Cultural tourist type	Motivation	Experience	Example from film-induced tourism
	Cultural tourism is...	The tourist...	
Purposeful cultural tourist	...the primary motivation for visiting a destination.	...has a deep cultural experience.	A fan visiting film location sites on a 'pilgrimage', e.g. travelling to Tunisia specifically to visit *Star Wars* locations.
Sightseeing cultural tourist	...a primary or major reason for visiting a destination.	...has a shallower experience.	Visiting film-related sites is part of a broader holiday, e.g. visiting *Lord of the Rings* sites during a holiday to New Zealand.
Serendipitous cultural tourist	...not a reason for the tourist's travel.	...ends up having a deep cultural tourism experience.	A chance encounter with a film-related site or tour taken on a whim stimulates a deep interest in the film, e.g. doing the *Sound of Music* tour in Salzburg.
Casual cultural tourist	...a weak motive for visiting a destination.	...has a shallow experience.	A visit to Universal Studios is just one activity on a 'sun, sand and sea' holiday in California.
Incidental cultural tourist	...not a reason for the tourist's travel.	...participates in some activities and has shallow experiences.	A tourist visiting the Yorkshire moors on a walking holiday takes a 'detour' to walk around some locations for *Last of the Summer Wine*.

becoming part of the community in the process. Others, meanwhile, simply ride a temporary wave of popularity which quickly disappears once attention on the film, anime or television drama has passed.

Beyond simple categorizations of strong and weak motivation, there are even more complex questions about what type of film may induce significant (marketable) levels of tourist behaviour. In the most comprehensive study of film location tourist behaviour to date, Roesch concludes:

> [T]here is no single decisive trigger for film location tourism. In most cases, it is a combination of factors that initiates a travel decision. These triggers may encompass: (1) an exposed attractive, identifiable and accessible location where one or more scenes have been shot on-site. (2) The exposed place is tied into an emotional story with intrinsic elements of drama or romance. (3) The storyline is either based on a true story or on a popular novel. (4) The film has become a classic or cult film and has been watched again and again.
>
> (Roesch 2009, p. 200)

Other factors include acting quality, vivid characterization and media exposure. However, in Roesch's analysis we see the key elements of a contents tourism approach: locations, stories, multi-use and deep engagement with the contents among fans are the key factors triggering tourism.

An alternative way of thinking about film-induced tourism is in terms of the movement of people. Following Beeton (2005), film-induced tourism (and also contents tourism) may be divided into 'on-location', namely visiting sites where films have been shot, and 'off-location', namely visiting theme parks, attending film festivals and going on studio tours. Film-induced tourism may also be categorized in terms of the generic tourism terms 'in-bound' and 'out-bound'.

This provides a useful framework within which to situate the case studies in this article series. In Japan, where there are strong and distinct markets for both imported (mainly Hollywood) and domestic films, the main patterns of contents tourism may be categorized as follows:

1) Japanese domestic tourism to foreign film sites: people who visit Tokyo Disneyland and Universal Studios (Osaka) or locations used in foreign film sites (for example, for *The last samurai* at Engyōji Temple in Himeji).[3]
2) Japanese domestic tourism to Japanese film sites: people who visit sites related to Japanese-produced films, television dramas or anime.
3) Japanese outbound tourism to sites of foreign films: the Japanese tourists who visit film-related sites on overseas trips (from theme parks in Hollywood to *Winter sonata* locations in South Korea).
4) Foreign inbound tourists visiting sites in Japanese-produced films: foreign fans of anime, films and television dramas who visit related sites on a trip to Japan.

5) Foreign inbound tourists visiting Japanese locations of domestically produced films: this phenomenon has been particularly evident in connection with the Chinese hit film *If you are the one* which sparked a Chinese tourism rush to Eastern Hokkaido in 2008.
6) Japanese outbound tourists visiting the foreign locations featured in Japanese-produced films.

The articles in this series focus primarily on the second category, namely visits by Japanese tourists to sites related to Japanese-produced films. We also focus on only two of the three main actors within film-induced tourism: the tourists themselves (in 'Otaku tourism and the anime pilgrimage phenomenon in Japan' and '*Rekijo*, pilgrimage and "pop-spiritualism"') and the communities hosting film sites or locations ('Contents tourism and local community response' and 'Taiga dramas and tourism'). The third main category of actor, tour providers and companies, is not featured. The series, therefore, does not attempt a comprehensive overview of film-induced tourism in Japan, but provides two pairs of complementary articles about fans and communities.

Popular culture and tourism policy

One of the primary reasons why contents tourism has attracted so much interest in Japan in recent years is that Japanese popular culture has developed a huge international fan base. This is driving many people's desire to visit Japan, and, as all academics working in Japanese studies departments know, it drives many students' desires to study about and study in Japan, too.

For many, the term 'Japanese popular culture' will generate images of manga, anime and J-pop. However, scholars, commentators and policy-makers — and not only in Japan — have struggled to articulate a broadly agreed definition of 'popular culture'. A report commissioned by the Ministry of Foreign Affairs of Japan (2006) on the use of 'pop culture' in cultural diplomacy is emblematic of this problem. They defined 'pop culture' (*poppu karuchā*) as 'culture produced in the everyday lives of ordinary people' (*ippan shimin ni yoru nichijō no katsudō de seiritsu shite iru bunka*), a definition which they admitted allowed forms categorized as 'traditional culture' by many, such as ukiyo-e, pottery and the tea ceremony, to be categorized as *poppu karuchā* along with anime and manga. '*Poppu*', in this usage, really means 'popular' as in 'of the people', which is slightly different from the vernacular usage of 'pop culture' in English, which tends toward culture that is 'light' rather than 'heavy' and 'liked by many people' rather than a 'niche' or 'cult' interest.

Definitional problems abound, therefore, but in this series of articles we are not so concerned with subjective distinctions between pop ('light' or 'low') and high culture, or even thresholds of popularity that allow us to say a form is 'liked by many people'. Instead, our priorities are, first, identifying works of Japanese popular culture that have triggered tourism and, second, analysing that touristic behaviour and its local impacts.

This series is also an attempt to fill a relatively conspicuous hole in the broader literature on Japanese popular culture. As Japanese popular culture has increased its global reach, scholars have sought to unlock the secrets of its appeal and assess its impact. A large literature has emerged, which may be divided into various sub-literatures: for example, popular culture as a form of soft power (Otmazgin and Ben-Ari 2012, Chua 2012); globalization and the export/reception of Japanese culture (Iwabuchi 2002, Yoshimoto, Tsai and Choi 2010); analysis of historical trends within Japanese popular culture (MacWilliams 2008); anthropological studies of fans (Azuma 2009, Ito, Okabe and Tsuji 2012); surveys of a particular media format (for example, Napier 2000 and Lamarre 2009 on anime); and surveys of a particular genre (Shamoon 2012 on girls' comics). Across the board, there are also numerous case studies or textual analyses of particular works. Thus far, however, the big frame has typically been 'media' or 'culture'. There has been relatively little attention in English on the linkage between popular culture contents and tourism, or the effects of popular culture on particular communities, although the case study of tourism by Japanese fans of the South Korean drama *Winter sonata* is now quite well known within the tourism literature (Chan 2007, Kim *et al.* 2007).

The potential of popular culture to trigger tourism to and thereby the revitalization of Japan's regions in an era of depopulation and economic stagnation (see Matanle and Rausch 2011) has not been lost on the Japanese government, which has taken an increasingly proactive role in the promotion of popular culture (see Choo 2012). The key year is 2002. Before then, the government had instigated many tourism campaigns, but few specifically focused on popular culture as a potential tourist resource. Then, Douglas McGray's (2002) extremely influential article 'Japan's gross national cool' coincided with *Spirited away*'s Oscar win (for best animated picture) and a declaration by Prime Minister Koizumi Junichirō that Japan was an 'intellectual-property based nation' (Arai 2005, p. 5). This latter comment signified a crucial shift away from the focus on manufacturing that had characterized the economic miracle in the second half of the twentieth century and placed the focus on Japan's creative industries. In 2003, there was a restatement of an ambitious target to attract 10 million international tourists a year to Japan by 2010, and the focus of national branding began the shift from traditional culture to a blend of traditional and pop culture. Mimicking the 'Cool Britannia' campaign in the UK, Japan started to be promoted with the slogan 'Cool Japan'.

Throughout the 2000s, a number of landmark government reports and initiatives pushed the agendas of nation branding and tourism promotion via popular culture. A government report (Ministry of Land, Infrastructure, Transport and Tourism *et al.* 2005) called on local authorities to use contents as part of their regional development plans. A significant reorganization of the institutional architecture took place in 2008 with the establishment of the Japan Tourism

Agency. Then, in 2010, the Creative Industries Promotion Office was created with bold plans to increase the global share of the culture industry. The government produced a booklet titled *Japan anime tourism guide* to provide information for pop culture fans visiting Japan, followed the next year by the *Japan anime map* and the *Cool Japan daily* blog (http://cooljapandaily.jp) in 2012.

Just over a decade after first turning its eyes towards the economic potential of popular culture, therefore, the Japanese government is placing a high priority on harnessing this potential. The 'Cool Japan Strategy' (Ministry of Economy, Trade and Industry 2012a) stated that Japan should 'acquire foreign demand amounting to 8 to 11 trillion yen (at present, only 2.3 trillion yen) from the 900 trillion-yen [projected global] market [for life and culture related industries in 2020]'. This report identified five product categories that might be harnessed: content, fashion, food, lifestyle and tourism.

The relevance of contents tourism, therefore, is that it is a cornerstone of Japan's economic plans for the coming decade and it is hoped by the government that contents, tourism and the two working in concert as contents tourism will generate massive additional revenues for Japan. The government has gone beyond thinking of contents as an export business, but rather now considers contents to be the first stage of a national strategy that invites tourists to visit Japan as the site where those contents originated. In a landmark report from 2012, the Ministry of Economy, Trade and Industry (METI) referred to Japan as the '*seichi*' (sacred site) to which fans would be welcomed on a 'pilgrimage' (Ministry of Economy, Trade and Industry 2012b, p. 29). The language of 'otaku tourism', as discussed in the first article by Okamoto Takeshi, has now been employed by the government. Furthermore, in June 2013, the Japan Tourism Agency (JTA), Japan National Tourism Organization (JNTO), METI and the Japan External Trade Organization (JETRO) issued a joint action plan, which also mentioned sacred sites, that formalized the connection between the contents export business and Japan's national tourism strategy (Japan Tourism Agency *et al.* 2013, p. 2). One visible form in English of this new direction is the official links between JNTO's 'Japan. Endless Discovery' campaign and the Tokyo Otaku Mode website, which, in June 2014, had a page promoting tours to Japan by its customers (http://otakumode.com/sp/visit_japan) linked to JNTO's website and social media accounts (Facebook and Twitter).

The four articles that follow, therefore, are published at a crucial turning point in Japanese national tourism strategy, and, through analysis of the issues surrounding contents tourism in the past two to three decades, give insights into the potential of and possible problems with this strategy in the coming years.

The structure of the special edition

There are four articles in this series. They are listed in Table 2 along with their key features divided into three categories: 1) actors/subjects, 2) media formats/contents, and 3) locations.

Table 2 The four articles in this series

Author	Article	Actors & themes	Media & contents	Locations
Okamoto Takeshi	Otaku tourism	Otaku; tourism as communication.	Anime, Internet; fiction.	Washimiya (Saitama), Toyosato (Shiga).
Sugawa-Shimada Akiko	*Rekijo*, pilgrimage and 'pop-spiritualism'	*Rekijo* (female history fans); pilgrimage, pop-spiritualism and fantasy.	Media mix (drama, anime, light novels, games); historical semi-fiction.	Multiple sites including Yamagata, Niigata, Sendai, Kyoto & Shikoku.
Yamamura Takayoshi	Contents tourism and local community response	Anime fans, local communities, copyright holders; relations between actors.	Anime; fiction.	Washimiya (Saitama)
Philip Seaton	Taiga dramas and tourism	Historical figures (Sakamoto, Hijikata) as tourist resources; economic impacts of drama-induced tourism.	Television drama; historical non-fiction.	Hakodate, Hino (Tokyo), Kyoto, Kochi.

The first two articles focus on fans: their travel behaviours, experiences and motivations. Okamoto's article looks at the male world of the otaku and his patterns of anime pilgrimage and communication in the internet age. Sugawa-Shimada's article about female history fans, or *rekijo*, focuses on female tourists whose interest in historical sites and figures has been driven by representations of history in popular cultural forms such as manga and light novels.

The third and fourth articles focus more on the business context. Yamamura's case study of fan-local community collaboration in Washimiya reveals the potential for local economic development through anime tourism, while Seaton's study of Taiga drama tourism (induced by NHK's flagship historical drama) attempts to quantify the massive economic impact of drama-induced tourism.

The second category, media format and contents, relates to the nature of the tourism drivers. In the articles by Okamoto and Yamamura the main drivers are fictional anime series that, crucially, are set in real and identifiable locations that may be visited by fans. The articles by Sugawa-Shimada and Seaton focus on historical contents and the tourism they induce to actual historical sites. This form of contents tourism overlaps significantly with pre-existing heritage tourism. As a result of historical contents appearing in popular films, dramas or anime, historical sites benefit from greater publicity and visitation rates. Seaton's article, however, focuses purely on a more-or-less-accurate television drama (although NHK Taiga dramas are frequently accused of taking liberties with the facts), while Sugawa-Shimada's article focuses on a diverse media mix (including anime, dramas, games and light novels) in which fantasy and invention are often liberally mixed with real historical events and characters.

The final category is locations. The articles in the series cover a wide range of geographical locations. They include various prefectures throughout Japan, the metropolises of Tokyo and Kyoto as well as small towns; and places with large pre-existing tourism industries (such as Hakodate) as well as some where there was none before a film triggered a tourism boom.

As already stated, these articles do not attempt a comprehensive overview of contents tourism in Japan. However, they are an attempt to further the theoretical potential of the concept of contents tourism to an international audience beyond Japan, and also to demonstrate the considerable potential for new avenues in the research of Japanese popular culture that focus not simply on how popular culture is produced or received, but how popular culture drives other forms of behaviour, such as tourism, in our increasingly mediatized society of the twenty-first century.

Notes

1. This phrase is credited to Roger Riley in his endorsement of the book on the back cover, but has become a common phrase of introduction to Beeton's work on the Internet.
2. *Kontentsu tsūrizumu* is sometimes written as 'content tourism' in official Japanese websites and the scholarly literature (see, for example, Otmazgin and Ben-Ari 2012). However, in this article series we prefer 'contents tourism', not only because it is closer in pronunciation to the Japanese term, but also because it captures better the plurality of contents (narratives, characters, locations, music and so on) that may drive touristic behaviour.
3. Many of the scenes for *The last samurai* were actually filmed in New Zealand, an example of the phenomenon of 'runaway locations', which are often used for reasons of cost or convenience. However, some scenes from *The last samurai* were shot at Engyōji Temple on the outskirts of Himeji, which advertises the fact that it was a location for the film on its website: http://www. shosha.or.jp/index.html (accessed 2 June 2014).

References

Arai, H., 2005. Intellectual property strategy in Japan. *International Journal of Intellectual Property: Law, Economy and Management*, 1, 5–12. Available from: http://www.ipaj.org/english_journal/pdf/Intellectual_Property_Strategy.pdf [Accessed 2 June 2014].

Azuma, H., 2009. *Otaku: Japan's database animals*, trans. J. E. Abel and S. Kono. Minneapolis: University of Minnesota Press.

Beeton, S., 2005. *Film-induced tourism*. Bristol: Channel View.

Beeton, S., Yamamura, T. and Seaton, P., 2013. The mediatisation of culture: Japanese contents tourism and pop culture. *In:* J. Lester and C. Scarles, eds. *Mediating the tourist experience: from brochures to virtual encounters*. Farnham: Ashgate, 139–54.

Chan, B., 2007. Film-induced tourism in Asia: a case study of Korean television drama and female viewers' to visit Korea. *Tourism, Culture & Communication*, 7 (3), 207–224.

Choo, K., 2012. Nationalizing 'cool': Japan's global promotion of the content industry. *In:* N. Otmazgin and E. Ben-Ari, eds. *Popular culture and the state in East and Southeast Asia*. Abingdon: Routledge, 147–61.

Chua, B. H., 2012. *Structure, audience and soft power in East Asian pop culture*. Hong Kong: Hong Kong University Press.

Ito, M., Okabe, D. and Tsuji, I., eds. 2012. *Fandom unbound: otaku culture in a connected world*. New Haven, CT: Yale University Press.

Iwabuchi, K., 2002. *Recentering globalization: popular culture and Japanese transnationalism*. Durham, NC: Duke University Press.

Japan Tourism Agency et al., 2013. Hōnichi gaikokujin zōka ni muketa kyōdō kōdō keikaku. Available from: http://www.mlit.go.jp/common/001001483.pdf [Accessed 2 June 2014].

Kim, S. S. et al., 2007. Effects of Korean television dramas on the flow of Japanese tourists. *Tourism Management*, 28 (5), 1340–1353.

Lamarre, T., 2009. *The anime machine: a media theory of animation*. Minneapolis: University of Minnesota Press.

MacWilliams, M., ed., 2008. *Japanese visual culture: explorations in the world of manga and anime*. New York: M. E. Sharpe.

Masubuchi, T., 2010. *Monogatari wo tabi suru hitobito: kontentsu tsūrizumu to wa nani ka*. Tokyo: Sairyūsha.

Matanle, P. and Rausch, A., 2011. *Japan's shrinking regions in the 21st century: contemporary responses to depopulation and socioeconomic decline*. Amherst, NY: Cambria Press.

McGray, D., 2002. Japan's gross national cool. *Foreign Policy*, 130 (May–June 2002), 44–54.

McKercher, B. and du Cros, H., 2009. *Cultural tourism: the partnership between tourism and cultural heritage management*. New York: Routledge.

Ministry of Economy, Trade and Industry, 2012a. Cool Japan strategy: modified version of the Interim Report submitted to the Cool Japan Advisory Council, September 2012. Available from: http://www.meti.go.jp/english/policy/mono_info_service/creative_industries/pdf/121016_01a.pdf [Accessed 1 October 2013].

Ministry of Economy, Trade and Industry, 2012b. Kontentsu sangyō no genjō to kongo no hatten no hōkōsei. Available from: http://www.meti.go.jp/policy/mono_info_service/contents/downloadfiles/121226-1.pdf [Accessed 2 June 2014].

Ministry of Foreign Affairs, 2006. Poppu karuchā no bunka gaikō ni okeru katsuyō ni kansuru hōkoku. Available from: http://www.mofa.go.jp/mofaj/annai/shingikai/koryu/h18_sokai/05hokoku.html [Accessed 2 June 2014].

Ministry of Land, Infrastructure, Transport and Tourism, the Ministry of Economy, Trade and Industry, and the Agency for Cultural Affairs, 2005. Eizō tō kontentsu no sakusei, katsuyō ni yoru chiiki shinkō no arikata ni kansuru chōsa hōkokusho. Available from: http://www.mlit.go.jp/kokudokeikaku/souhatu/h16seika/12eizou/12eizou.htm [Accessed 2 June 2014].

Napier, S. J., 2000. *Anime from Akira to Princess Mononoke: experiencing contemporary Japanese animation*. New York: Palgrave.

Otmazgin, N. and Ben-Ari, E., eds, 2012. *Popular culture and the state in East and Southeast Asia*. Abingdon: Routledge.

Roesch, S., 2009. *The experiences of film location tourists*. Bristol: Channel View.

Shamoon, D., 2012. *Passionate friendship: the aesthetics of girls' culture in Japan*. Hawai'i: University of Hawai'i Press.

Steinberg, M., 2012. *Anime's media mix: franchising toys and characters in Japan*. Minneapolis: Minnesota University Press.

Yamamura, T., 2011. *Manga, anime de chiiki shinkō*. Tokyo: Tokyo Hōrei Shuppan.

Yoshimoto, M., Tsai, E. and Choi, J., eds, 2010. *Television, Japan, and globalization*. Ann Arbor: Center for Japanese Studies, The University of Michigan.

Philip Seaton is a Professor in the International Student Center, Hokkaido University, where he is the convenor of the Modern Japanese Studies Program. He is the author of *Japan's contested war memories* (Routledge, 2007) and won the Daiwa Japan Forum Prize in 2006 for the article 'Reporting the 2001 textbook and Yasukuni Shrine controversies'.

Yamamura Takayoshi is a Professor in the Center for Advanced Tourism Studies, Hokkaido University, Japan. His main research interests are cultural tourism planning and media design, cultural resource management and heritage tourism studies. He is the author of *Community development through anime and manga* (*Anime, manga de chiiki shinkō*, Tokyo Hōrei Shuppan) and numerous other articles on heritage and pop culture tourism.

Otaku tourism and the anime pilgrimage phenomenon in Japan

TAKESHI OKAMOTO

Abstract: This article analyses one aspect of the emerging phenomenon of otaku tourism: travel by mainly male fans of otaku subculture to anime 'sacred sites' (the locations that feature in favourite anime). It starts by placing discussion of otaku culture in the discourse of postmodernity and elaborating on how otaku subculture is generating new forms of communication. Then, the origins and characteristics of anime pilgrimage are traced. The article concludes by explaining how otaku tourism and anime pilgrimage generate distinctive forms of communication both among fans and between fans and the communities that experience influxes of anime tourists.

Introduction

In recent years, the travel behaviour of otaku has gained increasing scholarly (for example Hasegawa and Midorikawa 2005, Masubuchi 2010, Yamamura 2011, Okamoto 2013) and media attention in Japan as a number of municipalities have seen surges in tourism after they featured in or were otherwise somehow connected to a popular anime film or series. Visiting sites related to anime films is called *anime seichi junrei* (anime pilgrimage) by fans in Japan. It is a form of travel behaviour closely related to film-induced tourism, literature tourism and other forms of media-induced tourism that in Japan are more commonly referred to under the blanket term 'contents tourism.' As described in the introductory article to this special edition, the language of anime tourism (with Japan itself as a 'sacred site' for fans) now permeates government policy documents; furthermore, there is a shift away from seeing Japanese popular culture as simply an export business and a shift towards seeing popular culture as a tourism resource that will encourage inbound tourism to Japan. Otaku tourism and anime pilgrimage, therefore, are core elements of the Japanese government's 'Cool Japan' strategy in the 2010s.

This article has two main aims. The first is to clarify the processes of anime pilgrimage within the broader context of otaku tourism. Otaku are primarily male fans of manga, anime and computer games, and *otaku tourism* refers to the broader touristic behaviour patterns of these fans of otaku subculture with a very strong and particular interest in their favourite series, characters or games. The second is to study *anime pilgrimage* (or anime tourism) as one form of otaku tourism and to explore how the travel behaviour of otaku creates new forms of interpersonal links and communication.

Similar to the types of popular culture-induced tourism described in a number of other articles in this special edition, anime pilgrimage has a longer history than the relatively recent increase in interest in the phenomenon might at first suggest. This article's principal argument is that a distinctive travel culture has emerged among otaku, and this travel culture is best revealed through exploring new forms of communication among fans and communities that have developed during the course of anime pilgrimages.

Communication in the modern age and its relationship with tourism

Throughout the 2000s, there was a rapid development and spread of communications technology in Japan. As indicated in Figure 1, the number of internet users rose from 11.55 million in 1997 to 94.62 million in 2010, a more than

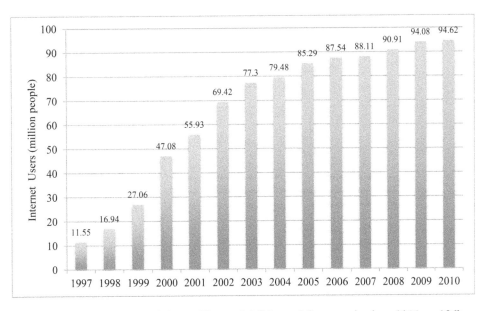

Figure 1 Internet users (Ministry of Internal Affairs and Communications 2011, p. 186)

eight-fold increase. The percentage of the population who were internet users rose from 9.2 per cent to 78.2 per cent. With approaching 80 per cent of the population using the internet, the extent of the 'internet age' becomes clear.

But it is not simply the number of internet users that is significant. Qualitative changes have been seen in the ways that people use the internet. This is evident in the 'u-Japan Policy' started by the Japanese government in May 2005, whose aim was: 'Working toward realizing the ubiquitous network society by 2010 in which "anyone can easily access and use a network anytime from anywhere and from any appliance"' (Ministry of Internal Affairs and Communications 2005). According to Tagami (2007, pp. 1–4), the u-Japan Policy meant the prioritization of people–people, people–thing and thing–thing communication, thereby precipitating a change from the previous emphasis on IT (information technology) to a new emphasis on ICT (information and communication technology), in other words using technology in communication.

With the spread of the internet and the new focus on communication in the use of information technology, debate has begun to take notice of these changes in the forms of communication and identities. For example, Tomita (2009) borrows the title of the 2004 French film and 2006 Hollywood remake *Intimate strangers* to describe a new form of relationship with others. An 'intimate stranger' is someone with whom one is intimate only via the media (Tomita 2009, p. 156), and the relationship is characterized by anonymity or secrecy. People who are anonymous and not intimate are simply 'others'; people who are not anonymous and with whom we are intimate are family and friends; while those who are not

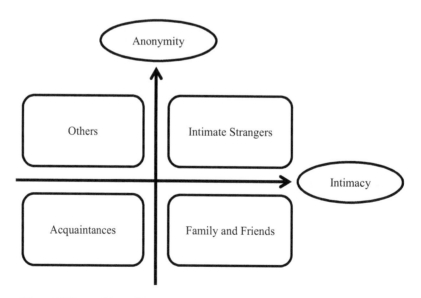

Figure 2 The position of intimate strangers. Based on Tomita (2009, p. 158)

anonymous but with whom we are not intimate are 'acquaintances'. Into this framework, represented in Figure 2, intimate strangers are a new form of 'others' who are anonymous yet intimate.

Individualism and avoiding others within reflexive modernity

In modern society, where tradition or the 'grand narratives' established by the community have less power than they used to, one must create values for oneself through one's own behaviour and choices. There is a change from the modern individual to the reflexive individual. Yamada (2009, p. 19), referring to the work of Giddens (1991), describes this as follows:

> With the progression of reflexive modernity, we are being released from the bonds of tradition or community. We freely choose our own lifestyles and have assumed more control over our own behaviour. Furthermore, with the system and basics of life that support a reflexive society already in place, we do not need to rely on others and it has become possible to live without caring too much about others. In this sort of society where individualization is advancing, we can think and act freely without the interference of others. But on the other hand, with the dilution of relationships with others within this process of individualization we feel a lack of places we are drawn to and tend to lose sight of the meanings of life.
>
> (Yamada 2009, p. 19)

People living in modern Japan feel less bound to tradition and community than they used to. People's choices have increased and the amount of information available to them is huge. Through the construction of a system by which individuals' qualities are judged, people are freed from tradition and community. But, with the emergence of this situation, individuals have had to take increasing responsibility themselves for various decisions. Society offers various opportunities, but turning these opportunities into success relies on the ability of the individual. With the individual having to take responsibility, the individual has to make choices and judgements. This means that one may live without relying on others or having them interfere in one's life, but it also means interfering in the lives of others less.

Formerly, society had the ability to establish a set of universal values referred to as a 'grand narrative' (Lyotard 1979), but this is being lost in Japanese society. Referring to the grand narrative, Azuma[1] writes:

> From the end of the eighteenth century to the mid-twentieth century in modern countries, various systems were consolidated for the purpose of organizing members of society into a unified whole; this movement was a precondition for the management of society. These systems became expressed, for instance, intellectually as the ideas of humanity and reason, politically as the nation-state

and revolutionary ideologies, and economically as the primacy of production. *Grand narrative* is a general term for these systems.

Modernity was ruled by the grand narrative. In contrast, in postmodernity the grand narratives break down and the cohesion of the social entirety rapidly weakens. In Japan that weakening was accelerated in the 1970s, when both high-speed economic growth and 'the season of politics' ended and when Japan experienced the Oil Shocks and the United Red Army Incident.

(Azuma 2009, p. 28)

In this way, the ability to create universal values ceases to function, and, as individualization progresses, the issue of how people find meaning in their lives has become an important one for modern Japanese society.

In tackling this issue, Azuma introduces the concept of 'database animals' (2009, pp. 25–95). Satisfying human emotions and meanings in life is not a matter of negotiation with others, but something one does on one's own. People undertake communication as a means of exchanging information, not of finding meaning. Azuma argues that this sort of lifestyle became prevalent after 1995, and he calls it 'The Animal Age'.

However, is it possible to find satisfaction in human emotions and meaning in life without negotiating with others and by acting individually? In principle, this is difficult because one needs to refer to others in order to establish one's own identity and to find meaning in life. What is indisputable, though, is that the way we are relating to others is changing. This can be seen in the emergence of 'intimate strangers' and the decline of the 'grand narrative', and it raises the question of what sort of relationships can be built. In attempting to answer this question, Yamada (2011) distils the arguments of Azuma (2001) and Uno (2008) in the following way.

Whether it is a community in cyberspace or in the real space of a political group, 'island universes' [*shima uchū*] are exclusive communities made up of people who believe in small narratives and share values with other members. People who possess different value systems are completely excluded as 'noise'. For this reason, colleagues in the island universes are 'others', but 'others' who have had their extreme otherness blanked out. In other words, through otherness being thoroughly concealed, the avoidance of others is undertaken. Azuma states that database animals can live while avoiding others, and describes this as an appropriate strategy in the database consumption postmodern condition. But Uno, criticizing Azuma, argues that contrary to Azuma's predictions, as we have entered the twenty-first century the 'decolorization of otherness' strategy has led to the creation of excluded communities, and society today is suffering from the logic and violence of that exclusion.

(Yamada 2011, p. 11)

In other words, because it is difficult to reconstitute the lost 'grand narrative', groups of like-minded people gather together and produce 'small narratives' that give meaning to them as individuals. Belief in these small narratives is shared with groups of like-minded others in 'island universes'. For the small narrative to be believed, the values must be valid within the 'island universe'. The 'grand narrative' no longer exists, so people must construct meanings themselves that give power to the 'little narrative'. One strategy for achieving this is the exclusion of other values. First, people raise the purity of their own values, and then by increasing intimacy within the 'island universe' they can create a 'little narrative'.

But this is where a problem arises. There is nothing that guarantees the value of the small narrative. There is no grand narrative to supply meaning to individuals. Whenever values clash, one's values are compared to others, and, in order to give power to the values that one believes in, the strategy is to assert difference. In this way, island universes with their small narratives take on an exclusivity and it can be assumed that they engage in competition with each other. In fact, this situation has been described in terms of the diversification of values within modern Japanese society (Okamoto 2013, pp. 20–21). People gravitate towards others who share similar values and small narratives. Meanwhile, 'others possessing otherness' are excluded and ignored within this system of communication.

Is tourism a solution for these issues?

This article considers whether tourism, and particularly otaku tourism, is a means for resolving the situation described thus far by creating a cycle of encounters with 'others possessing otherness'.

First it is necessary to define some terms, particularly 'others possessing otherness' (*tashasei wo motta tasha*). As long as people live within society, it is very difficult for them to live their lives without coming across other others. People share their homes with family members. Family members, in this sense, are 'others'. Even those who live on their own will come across people they do not know when they venture outside. These are also 'others'. But, in the argument thus far, the issue has not been that people do not meet 'others' at all. The issue has been as one 'other' forms a relationship with another 'other', otherness is removed and we choose to interact with others possessing low levels of otherness. In other words, whether the person has the same interests or enjoys the same contents, we choose others with whom we have been able to confirm 'sameness' and develop relationships with them. When differences are discovered with these others, we avoid the differences. However, 'others possessing otherness' are those with whom commonality cannot be guaranteed.

It has been hypothesized that tourism has the function of enabling encounters with 'others possessing otherness' (see, for example, Yamada 2008, Yoshida 2008, Endo 2010). Endo (2010) theorizes that the superficial elements of fun and play within tourism are actually important for the construction of the public sphere (*kōkyōken*). In this sense, Endo describes the public sphere as follows.

> The public sphere is not a 'community' underpinned by common identity where people share similar values. Even if people do not share the same values they are able to enter the public sphere, and even if they do not share the same values with others, they are able to exchange feelings, opinions and thoughts in an atmosphere of mutual respect. This is the essence of the public sphere.

(Endo 2010, p. 36)

In other words, tourism does not take place in 'island universes' (or 'community' in Endo's terminology) and it does not involve only the members of an 'island universe' group ('people who share the same values') who share a particular small narrative. Tourism has the potential to create a space where people can meet 'others possessing otherness'. If this is the case, society does not simply value commonality, or sharing the same narrative, but through tourism a society allowing differentness and multiple narratives becomes possible (Endo 2010, p. 37).

This is the potential of tourism in theory, although the extent to which this kind of space generated by tourism is actually possible is open to debate. To explore whether it is possible in practice, I will analyse otaku tourism, and specifically anime pilgrimage.

Otaku and the development of anime tourism

The term '*otaku*' (literally 'your house') was coined in 1983. The development of the otaku phenomenon is closely related to the development of the media. Namba has traced the history of media liked by the '*otaku zoku*' (otaku tribe) from the 1960s to 1980s, when they were called mania, hardcore fans or 'nekura tribe' (Namba 2007, pp. 247–248). Otaku subculture had its roots in the science fiction novels in the 1960s, but it was the development of video games, anime, television programmes, comic markets, magazines, computers and video players that underpinned the development of otaku culture. In 1989, the rape and murder of a number of young girls by an otaku (the Miyazaki Tsutomu case; see Azuma 2009, pp. 4–5) gave otaku culture notoriety and made the term widely known. Since the 1990s, the arrival of the digital age has meant the diversification of otaku culture and otaku have lost their previous cohesion as a 'tribe' (Namba 2007, p. 259). As we shall see a little later, anime pilgrimage, the main subject of this article, is a form of otaku behaviour that began in the 1990s.

The social commentator Azuma Hiroki has analysed the consumer behaviour of otaku, the products they consume and their postmodern characteristics. In *Otaku: Japan's database animals* he says otaku is 'a general term referring to those who indulge in forms of subculture strongly linked to anime, video games, computers, science fiction, special-effects films, anime figurines, and so on' (Azuma 2009, p. 3). In other words, the definition revolves around the objects of their interest.[2] The sociologist Osawa Masachi has argued that, from the second half of the 2000s, the personality traits of otaku have been considered an ordinary phenomenon among young people (Osawa 2008, p. 86). In other words, while otaku have diversified they have also become more mainstream. Rather than limiting the definition of otaku to the type of person, therefore, it is more appropriate to define otaku according to the objects of their interests. Hence, in this article I use Azuma's definition of otaku.

As we have seen, the scale and nature of otaku culture have changed over time. Azuma (2009, pp. 6–7) identifies three otaku generations. The first generation comprises mainly those born around 1960 who grew up watching *Space Battleship Yamato* and *Mobile Suit Gundam* in their teens. The next generation was born around 1970. They spent their teens consuming the otaku culture of the previous generation, which had achieved maturity and split into various subcultures. The third generation was born around 1980 and was in high school around the time of the *Neon Genesis Evangelion* boom (around 1997).

Anime tourism began in the 1990s. Consequently, this article concentrates mainly on the third generation, which has two main characteristics. First, they have an easy familiarity with modern communications technology. As Azuma (ibid.) states, this generation was in its teens when the internet became part of everyday life. They send or collect information via the internet, or make computer graphics, and as a result their patterns of communication, expression and consumption differ greatly from those of previous generations.

This third generation avidly transmits and collects information. One example is *dōjinshi*, or fan-produced magazines.[3] In otaku culture, *dōjinshi* are published in great numbers and borrow worldviews or characters from favourite anime. Fan-produced materials also include books, tapes or CDs, floppy disks or CD-ROMs, videos, figures, characters and other goods (Kobayashi 1999). These are exchanged and sold at comic markets and other events. In these *dōjinshi* and other derivative works, the already existing media texts (the original contents) are reinterpreted and reproduced by fans. Fans fill in the gaps in stories, interpret the metaphors and storylines or even combine the contents with elements of other publications (Murase 2003). The interpretations may differ from the original intentions of the contents producers, and the fans become an active audience that transmits its interpretations of the contents.

This kind of information collection and re-transmission has developed alongside advances in communications technology and is particularly evident on the internet. Representative examples are derivative videos or images, such as MAD and 'fan subs'. MAD (derived from 'MAD tape', an early form of cassette tape) is when an existing video, soundtrack, game or anime is edited and recreated. 'Fan sub' is shorthand for 'fan subtitles' and refers to the addition of foreign-language subtitles to videos by fans so that the contents may be enjoyed by fans abroad, too. These videos are placed on video-sharing sites such as YouTube and Nikoniko dōga. In some of the 'fan sub' videos seen by the author, it is not only subtitles that have been added, but also commentary in foreign languages about some of the unexplained aspects of Japanese culture in the videos, for example what tatami mats or kendo are.

With such MAD or 'fan sub' videos, as well as with *dōjinshi* and other derivative works, there is a copyright issue. However, interesting fan-produced materials may create word-of-mouth publicity for the original contents and attract even more fans to the original works. Scouts on the lookout for promising new contents creators also actively look through derivative works. The 'fan sub' genre also has the potential to open up foreign markets to the original contents. In all of these ways, members of the third generation of otaku, with their deep familiarity with the internet, are very active in transmitting information.

The second characteristic of the third generation of otaku is that its behaviour exhibits postmodern characteristics. Azuma argues that 'database consumption' is a form of postmodern consumer behaviour and that the characteristics of 'animalization' (*dōbutsuka*) are evident in patterns of otaku 'database consumption'.

For Azuma, the consumption of a particular work is 'not simply to consume a work (a small narrative) or a worldview behind it (a grand narrative), nor to consume characters and settings (a grand nonnarrative). Rather it is linked to consuming the database of otaku culture as a whole. I call this consumer behavior *database consumption*' (2009, p. 54). He explains this in terms of '*chara-moe*' (*chara* means character, *moe* refers to an empathy or adoration for). *Chara-moe* grows in otaku according to the 'combination of *moe*-elements' that are extracted from the database. Among otaku, communication with others is based on information exchange, and their interest in that social interaction is based on their interest only in a particular set of information.

It is these forms of consumption and communication that give rise to the characteristics of animalization. Animalization is when 'each person closes various lack–satisfaction circuits' (ibid., p. 87). In other words, when people feel they lack something, they try to achieve satisfaction without the need for the existence of others or without interacting with others. This pattern of gaining satisfaction is increasing.

Tendencies to join 'island universes' or exclusiveness have been confirmed within otaku. But this does not mean that otaku never have contact with others. They gather at comic markets where people share the same interests and they are extremely active in transmitting information to others. Furthermore, otaku may meet up in real (as opposed to virtual) spaces with those possessing similar interests whom they have met online, a practice which is called *ofukai*, or 'offline meeting'.

Broadly speaking, *ofukai* are when the members of communities who have formed intimate relationships online actually meet in person. These *ofukai* meetings may take place anywhere. People who like singing anime songs might meet in a karaoke box, for example. In *ofukai*, the most important thing is the links people share through their common interests. In other words, it is vibrant communication in 'island universes' where people share the same values and interests.

The question of most relevance to understanding otaku tourism, however, is what happens when otaku go as tourists to places where they are bound to meet 'others possessing otherness'. We can explore examples of precisely this situation by looking at the phenomenon of anime pilgrimage.

The beginnings of anime pilgrimage

Anime pilgrimage is defined as visiting sites depicted in anime, games, manga and other forms of otaku culture. Even though the term 'pilgrimage' has religious connotations, there is no particular link with religion. The term is used here primarily because it is the term that otaku use themselves to describe their own behaviour. Places of particular significance to anime fans have become known as 'sacred sites' (*seichi*) and the act of visiting sacred sites is called 'pilgrimage' (*seichi junrei*). A detailed comparison with other forms of pilgrimage is beyond the scope of this article and some commentators have discussed the inherent religiosity of anime or pop-culture pilgrimage.[4] But in this article the term 'anime pilgrimage' is used simply to refer to visitations to sites of importance for anime fans.

Determining when anime pilgrimage began means answering two separate questions: when the term 'anime pilgrimage' began to be used, and when the practices now referred to as anime pilgrimage began. Judging by the results of a survey of mainstream media sources, 'anime pilgrimage' began gaining attention in 2008. On 2 March 2009, I searched for articles over the entire period of the So-net online news database[5] (which carries the major daily newspapers in digital format from the mid-1980s) using the keywords 'anime' and 'seichi junrei'. After removing all articles not related to anime pilgrimage as defined in this article, a total of eighteen articles remained. There was one in 1995, one in 2003, one in 2007, eleven in 2008 and four in 2009. The year 2008 seems to be when the term attracted widest media attention and thus broadly entered popular consciousness.

Yet the practice clearly predates 2008, and use of the term '*seichi junrei*' in mainstream media has also lagged behind its use within the otaku community. In the introduction to his 2005 book *Seichi junrei: anime, manga, 12-kasho meguri* ('Twelve sites of anime and manga pilgrimage'), Kakizaki (2005, pp. 4–5) describes visiting sites in 1995 on the Japan Railways Iida Line that featured in the anime *Kyūkyoku Chōjin R* (an 'original video animation', OVA, sold by Bandai Visual in 1991). Kakizaki also mentions visiting Tarō Shrine in Okayama prefecture, which appeared in the 1992 OVA *Tenchi Muyō!* It is clear that fans were visiting the shrine on a 'pilgrimage' and that they interacted to some extent with local people. However, Kakizaki does not say whether the travel behaviour was called 'anime pilgrimage' at the time.

Meanwhile, Fujiyama (2006, p. 218) writes that some of the oldest instances of anime pilgrimage date from the time of *Sailor moon*, which was broadcast on television between 1992 and 1997. During the traditional first shrine visits of the year (*hatsumōde*) there were long queues of fans at Hikawa Shrine in Azabujuban, Tokyo, which appeared in the anime.

Finally, Hashimoto (2006, pp. 178–180) discusses how the light novel *Mirage of blaze* by Kuwabara Mizuna induced a lot of travel by young women to the Uesugi festival in the early 1990s. This episode is described in detail by Sugawa-Shimada Akiko in another article in this issue.

Putting together all this evidence, one may conclude that clear examples of anime pilgrimage existed by the early 1990s, although the term 'anime pilgrimage' was not commonly used then. However, the term was being used in otaku circles well before the mainstream media started using the term more regularly after 2008.

The motivations of anime pilgrims

The desire to undertake anime pilgrimage begins with the viewing of anime. But if the fan simply views the anime and is unable to access information about the locations featured in the anime, the fan has no way of knowing where to visit. When fans have obtained information about locations, including those that actually exist, then anime pilgrimage can begin.

Information may be divided into 'known' and 'acquired'. 'Known' information refers to that which is already part of the fan's knowledge. When a previously seen and recognized place appears as a location in an anime, the existence of the location is quickly confirmed. 'Acquired knowledge' is when the fan learns of the location by word of mouth, over the internet or from media and other sources.

Based on differences in the ways in which fans have obtained information about locations, we can identify three types of anime pilgrimage. The first is pioneer pilgrimage. The pioneers are the people who, after watching the anime, work out where the locations are. Based on my interviews with pioneer pilgrims, they use various forms of information to identify the locations: these include landmarks or geographical features in the background scenery, information from novels on which the anime was based, other materials such as photos, information about the home towns of the directors or scriptwriters and road signs or stations that appear in the anime. Then, using internet tools such as Google Street View or Yahoo Maps, they find the precise locations. Many pioneers refer to this practice of seeking out and visiting locations as '*butai tanbō*', literally 'finding and visiting the stage'.

The second type of pilgrimage is undertaken based on the information posted on the internet by the pioneers. When pilgrims arrive at the locations, they carry with them printouts of the pioneers' websites and blogs or check the locations on the internet using mobile devices.

The third type of pilgrimage is undertaken by people who have obtained information about the locations from the news or mass media. Many instances of anime pilgrimage go unnoticed by the media, but sometimes the pilgrimage attracts sufficient attention to make them mainstream news. Whatever the type of anime pilgrimage, the fundamental motivation of travellers is to visit the sites that appear in anime.

Finding information about anime pilgrimage

There are two main sources of travel information for anime pilgrims: organizations, such as companies and/or local authorities, and individuals, whether pilgrims or local residents.

Much information is provided by organizations such as travel agents, hotels, companies holding the copyright for the anime, local government, tourism associations and local trade associations. Anime pilgrims seek out information on transport, accommodation and other tourism infrastructure in much the same way as other tourists. There are few guidebooks published about anime pilgrimage sites, although some do exist, for example *Twelve locations of anime and manga pilgrimage* (Kakizaki 2005), *Moe rurubu Cool Japan – the Otaku Japan guide* (JTB Publishing 2008) and *Anime and comics pilgrimage navi* (Drill Project 2010). There are also tour packages offered by travel agents, such as tours to take part in a specific anime-related event, but none is offered on a regular basis. Anime pilgrims tend to travel individually or in small groups, and group tours are rare.

The second source of travel information is individuals, either pilgrims or members of the local community, who post information on blogs or homepages. On the social networking service mixi there are communities for many individual anime films, and social networking services (SNS) are also a useful way for fans to exchange information. There are various fan communities and some have more than 1,000 members. Sometimes people living in the anime locations are also members. One such example is Washimiya, discussed in the article by Yamamura Takayoshi. In this case, the local traders' association even put notifications of new anime-related products on internet notice-boards so that they can gain feedback from fans.

Such patterns of information exchange differ from traditional forms of information exchange between tourist, agent and destination. The information flows go in two directions. Previously, tourist destinations or travel agents would mainly send publicity about their tourist resources in one direction to potential tourists. Or, in other forms of contents tourism, such as Taiga drama-induced tourism (the subject of the article in this issue by Philip Seaton) the drama itself provides much information about locations, either in a segment at the end of the programme that lists locations and/or related sites or in spin-off publications such as magazines.

However, the particular characteristic of anime tourism is the incalculable volume of information being exchanged among tourists, and the extent to which travellers are also active in telling local communities their views too. Some fans read the pilgrimage journals of others and then embark on a pilgrimage to the sacred site themselves; people read the journals online and ask questions of the authors; and I have seen during my own visits to sacred sites that many pilgrims carry printouts of fan sites with them when they go travelling. Such trends are increasingly being seen across the tourism industry in the internet age, but they have been a conspicuous aspect of anime pilgrimage from the outset of the phenomenon.

The touristic behaviour of anime pilgrims

Based on my observations during extensive fieldwork among fans on anime pilgrimages, broadly speaking we can identify six particular forms of otaku behaviour among anime pilgrims. Not all anime pilgrims exhibit all six forms of behaviour (and many people who do not consider themselves otaku might do similar things), but they may all be called particularly characteristic of otaku tourism.

The first is that fans take photographs of the locations they visit from the same angles that the places are shown in the anime. Many take pictures with direct reference to the original contents and compare their photos with the originals. Fans may take figurines from the anime with them and photograph them against the background. Photographs may not only be of views that would normally be considered photogenic, such as shrines or scenic viewpoints, but may be of places of little intrinsic or photographic interest to others who are not fans of the anime, such as a car-park or a station (see Figure 3). Such filmic re-enactments are a common feature of many forms of film location tourism (see Roesch 2009, pp. 162–164).

The second form of behaviour is that travellers leave mementoes or evidence of their trips such as objects, comments or illustrations. Particular examples include comments or illustrations in pilgrimage notebooks, drawings of scenes or characters from the anime on *ema* votive plaques hung in shrines, and leaving anime goods purchased in the pilgrimage site or their own original illustrations. The pilgrimage notebooks are sometimes created by the fans themselves, while on other occasions they are created by the host communities and left in restaurants, stations or tourist offices. Such fan notebooks have been found in a number of anime pilgrimage sites including Washimiya (*Lucky star*) and Toyosato (*K-On*).

(a)

(b)

Figure 3 (a) Recreating a scene from *Lucky star* at Kasukabe Station, Saitama prefecture;[6] (b) A nondescript 'sacred site': bicycle park in Nishinomiya, Hyogo prefecture (*The melancholy of Haruhi Suzumiya*)[7]

In the notebook at Washimiya, for example, pilgrims signed their names, drew illustrations, said how many times they had visited, wrote comments about the places they had visited, gave their thoughts about the anime, said where they were from and whether they were planning to visit again (Okamoto 2008).

The third is that fans take laptop computers or mobile phones with them and provide live updates or pilgrimage diaries in real time on internet notice-boards, blogs or video sites like YouTube. Such online postings may also be done after the pilgrimage is over. In the internet and Facebook age, posting travel pictures online as you go may be considered a very normal sort of behaviour, but in the context of otaku tourism the point is that a person who does *not* do this would be quite unusual.

The fourth form of behaviour is decorating cars with anime stickers and illustrations. Such cars are called *itasha*. The term *itasha* is derived from otaku humour. The cars look *itaitashii* (painful, in the sense of embarrassing), but at the same time *itasha* is the same term as for an Italian-made car, so it has the ironic nuance of being upmarket too. The practice of decoration with anime stickers can also be seen on bicycles, motorbikes and other vehicles. The interiors of cars may also be decorated with figurines, cushions and other anime goods.

The fifth form of behaviour is cosplay: dressing up in the costumes and appearances of anime characters. Cosplay is not limited to characters of the cosplayer's gender: men may dress as female characters and vice versa. Cosplayers may be seen at events that range in size from huge international conventions to small-scale events held in sacred sites. Often these events are organized by municipalities and cosplaying is permitted only within the venue. However, cosplayers may also be seen in public as part of promotional events, particularly when the town is actively welcoming fans as part of its anime tourism promotional activities. For example, in Chichibu, Saitama prefecture, location of the anime series *The flower we saw that day*, a local newspaper report shows fans posing with a cosplayer at the local train station next to a train with a picture from the anime on the front of the train (Saitama Shinbun 2011).

The sixth form of behaviour is the acceptance of interaction between traveller and host community, and among fellow travellers. It is very common to see anime pilgrims in conversation with local people at sites of pilgrimage. There is also considerable interaction among pilgrims. But this can vary according to the location. As mentioned above, there are some anime pilgrimage sites in nondescript urban spaces such as car parks. There is typically little interaction between pilgrims and local communities or other fans in such sites. But in locations where the pilgrims may stay in the community, there may be interaction between pilgrims and locals.

In many instances, the relationship is positive. An influx of visitors to a locality can bring economic benefits and other forms of community revitalization, so many towns welcome pilgrims. In Chichibu, for example, the Chichibu Anime Tourism Executive Committee estimated that 80,000 fans of *The flower we saw that day* had visited the town in 2011, generating 320 million yen (Saitama Shinbun 2011). And the best-known example of an extremely positive relationship created between fans and the local community is the case of Washimiya, described in the article by Yamamura Takayoshi.

However, the relationship is not always so smooth. Some localities and communities that have featured in anime have expressed concerns. Kanda (2012) writes that some members of the community in the location for the anime *Higurashi when they cry*, Shirakawa in Gifu Prefecture, said that the image of their community created was 'not the real Shirakawa'. In other words, they were unhappy with the way that their community had been represented. Shirakawa is an immaculately preserved old village famous for its thatched roof houses and is a UNESCO World Heritage Site. But the anime was a murder mystery story and this was not the type of image that locals wanted created for their town.

Other communities feel uncomfortable with the influx of fans. Kanda (ibid.) reports that members of some communities have complained that fans visiting their town in cosplay do not fit in with the atmosphere of the community. In other words, they have no issues with people cosplaying or driving around in *itasha* cars in major cities or secluded spaces, but they feel uncomfortable when such activities occur in their communities. On occasions, there have been incidents of a more serious nature. For example, the location of the anime *The melancholy of Haruhi Suzumiya*, Nishinomiya Senior High School, experienced incidents of trespassing by fans, leading the school to call on fans to behave appropriately.

As can be seen from these examples, when a location appears in an anime and this results in anime pilgrimage, there are opportunities for conflict to arise between groups of people with differing values. However, there are also occasions on which, through mutual cooperation, a positive relationship can be forged between community and fans.

Post-pilgrimage behaviour

As has been described, otaku are very active in information dissemination. There are three primary forms of information dissemination by pilgrims during or after their visits: via the internet, in the real space of the site of pilgrimage and among circles of friends and acquaintances.

Pilgrims post information about their trips on homepages, blogs, SNS community pages or notice-boards. Many pilgrims publish 'pilgrimage journals' online including photographs or videos that they have taken in the sacred site. In September 2013, one of these sites (http://legwork.g.hatena.ne.jp/) contained an online archive of over 1,000 diaries listing visits to sacred sites related to manga, anime, novels, games and light novels.

There are sites in which the photos taken by the tourists are published alongside images from the anime for comparison. During my interviews with the producers of such sites, they said that they use information from the internet (such as Google Earth) as well as visits by bicycle or on foot around the location to obtain detailed information. Many of these sites have a huge following. The website Butai Tanbō Matome (http://wiki.livedoor.jp/lsh_er/), for example, receives around 850,000 hits per year. Many pilgrims post videos online, too. There are many anime pilgrimage videos to be seen on video sites such as YouTube or Nikoniko dōga. In one such example, a live action version of the opening scenes of the anime *K-On* filmed on location was produced by fans and uploaded to YouTube.[8]

In all these types of online activity, consideration is usually shown to the people from the site of pilgrimage. For example, if people or their vehicles (number plates) appear in the photographs, the photos may be altered so that the individuals cannot be identified. If private residences are involved, the locations are concealed. There is a sort of code of conduct among anime pilgrims that all photos from the sacred sites should in no way cause *meiwaku* (harm or inconvenience) to the people in the local communities. The reason for this attitude is negative feelings toward otaku that otaku have often seen or felt themselves. On various occasions, I have heard comments that people are afraid that, if they cause trouble to local communities, fans will no longer be able to go on pilgrimages.

The second form of post-pilgrimage behaviour is information transmission in the offline world. Some pilgrims make guidebooks about the locations at their own expense (see Figure 4); some produce *dōjinshi* which are distributed at comic markets or exchanged among fans. Fan-produced materials may even be found at shops in the locations themselves. Sometimes these publications are produced for more altruistic motives. Yamamura (2011, pp. 90–91) presents a transcribed interview in which the author of one such publication explains how helping out fellow fans on a pilgrimage to sites related to the anime *Lucky star* was a reason for his activities. Other fans, meanwhile, have shown concern for the locality. In one fan-produced guidebook that I have seen about the anime *K-On*, the author wrote a detailed manga history of the old Toyosato elementary school buildings where the anime was set.[9]

Such fan activities are not just limited to Japanese tourists. One pilgrim from Hong Kong whom I met at the location of *Please teacher* in Nagano Prefecture had been to Japan several times and was involved in the production of guidebooks in both Japanese and Chinese. There is also a market for such fan-produced literature outside Japan. This traveller also recounted how he talked about his experiences to friends and sometimes returned to Japan with different travel partners. Through such examples, we can see that anime tourism and otaku tourism is not simply a Japanese phenomenon but has international dimensions too.

The third and final form is when fans talk to their friends or revisit sites with different friends. In this sense, anime pilgrimage is no different from other forms of tourism. In August and September 2009 I visited four sites of anime pilgrimage and distributed questionnaires to fans to ask where they obtained their information about sacred sites (Okamoto 2010). Out of the 1,189 people who

Figure 4 Fan-produced guidebooks

responded, the commonest answer was the internet (42.4 per cent) followed by 'from acquaintances' (24.3 per cent). Other information sources included television news (8.8 per cent) and books/magazines (6.2 per cent). Another survey conducted by the Japan Travel and Tourism Association (2010) also placed people (in this case 'family and friends') in second place with 36.4 per cent. The precise percentages vary, perhaps according to different question wordings and other survey conditions, but direct people-to-people communication is clearly an important element when planning and undertaking anime tourism.

Forms of fan: community communication

While on an anime pilgrimage, fans may use various forms of self-expression, such as drawing and writing messages on *ema* votive plaques or decorating cars (*itasha*), that mark them as otaku tourists. In this way, people in the local communities realize that anime fans are visiting their communities. Sites of anime pilgrimage are often residential areas that would not normally expect to have any tourists. Consequently, there are many instances in which local people do not even realize that their neighbourhood has become a tourist site. However, when local people become aware of the fact that anime fans are visiting their communities, dialogue and interaction with the fans may begin. Through that dialogue, a tourism culture involving many different actors is built from the bottom up.

One of the most important examples of this is in Washimiya, which was the location of the anime *Lucky star* (see the article by Yamamura Takayoshi). Another example of positive collaboration is the town of Toyosato in Saga prefecture, site of the anime *K-On*. Since June 2010, the standard road signs warning motorists that children might jump into the road have been replaced with ones featuring characters from the anime (Figure 5). There are signs featuring different characters at various places in the town. The original idea for, and production of, the signs came from fans with the help of the local community.

Furthermore, in the old buildings of Toyosato elementary school (Figure 6b), the model for the high school that the main characters in the anime went to, there is a tourist site created by fans. *K-On* is about the daily life of a group of high school girls in the light music club. In the anime there are many scenes where the girls sit down to have tea together using expensive crockery. Some anime fans are known as *tokuteichū*, fans who seek out the real identities of objects that appear in the anime (they are close relatives of the pioneers who seek out the locations). The *tokuteichū* post the information on the internet when they have discovered the identities of the objects. In the case of Toyosato, anime pilgrims who had seen information about the crockery in the anime bought an actual set of the same crockery and plastic replicas of the sweets and placed them in the school buildings of the old Toyosato elementary school. This scene is shown in Figure 6a.

As we can see, in the communities where anime pilgrimage takes place there are many ways to link the locality – its festivals, culture, scenery or buildings – and

Figure 5 *K-On*-inspired road signs in Toyosato

anime culture or otaku culture. This combination itself becomes the contents which people come to see and enjoy. This phenomenon turns on its head traditional notions of host and guest because fans visiting the communities create spaces, events or objects that are enjoyed by the local community and other visitors. This is the bottom-up creation not simply of tourism information, but tourism culture itself.

Furthermore, through repeated visits some anime pilgrims have come to see the wider value of interaction with the local community and residents. Among pilgrims who visited Toyosato, for example, there are those who were simply interested in the elementary school as the location of the anime *K-On*. But they came to appreciate other local buildings and visit them, too.

There are even examples of fans who have moved to anime sacred sites or found work there. In a conversation with one fan of *K-On* who had moved to Toyosato, he explained that he first visited the town after watching the anime, but thereafter he built relationships with various people in the town and Toyosato assumed a more important position in his life. This was why he decided to move there. There were principally two types of people he met there. The first type was anime fans and sacred site pilgrims. The second was people who lived in the locality. In this way, he possessed a hybrid network of acquaintances not simply formed through a shared interest in the contents and facilitated by the internet, but formed in the real space of the anime sacred site.

(a)

(b)

Figure 6 (a) The tea set from *K-On*; (b) Toyosato Elementary School

While the internet plays a vital role in otaku tourism, it is very difficult to form links with local communities simply through communication over the internet. Of course, if there are people in the locality who are well versed in online communication such links may be formed. But that would mean that only local people who understood the values of the online community could interact with the anime pilgrims. It is inconceivable that all residents of a sacred site are also members of online communities that discuss the site. This would mean the opening up of the 'island universe' to those with other values, and it is debatable whether this is ever possible. In other words, tourism, the act of visiting a particular place, is what allows the links between fans and local communities to be formed.

Among anime pilgrims, many fans call each other by their online user names. This is a largely anonymous form of communication. During my fieldwork, I have witnessed many instances of pilgrims using their real names, although there are also many fans who use their online user names when on pilgrimage. In the latter case, local people call the pilgrims by their user names, too. The user name is used for a more anonymous form of communication. Of course, if the interaction took place only in the virtual world, it would be completely anonymous and easier to cut off the relationship. But with anime pilgrimage, even if pilgrims use a user name, they have gone in person to visit a site in the real world and their existence can be confirmed. Even if the person's real name is not known, others will have memories of his face; and, even if the user name changes, as long as the person's appearance does not change too much the relationship can continue. It might be anonymous and the relationship might be based on incomplete disclosure of basic personal information, but nonetheless the existence of the person has been confirmed. This is another distinctive form of fan–fan and fan–community communication created by otaku tourism.

Conclusions

This article has sought to define and explain the processes of anime pilgrimage through a particular focus on distinctive forms of communication that have emerged within otaku tourism. Anime pilgrimage is tourism starting with the exhaustive pursuit of an interest. Using modern information technology, information is collected from a 'database' created by the bottom-up participation of a wide variety of actors. As a result of increased pilgrimage by people sharing the same interest, the effects become visible in real communities. There are increasing opportunities for people in local communities and pilgrims (or even those whose travel purpose is not pilgrimage) to interact with each other. There are some communities where this interaction is quite sustained. As a result of visiting the localities, the pilgrims' opportunities to experience other forms of local culture increase. Through repeated mutual effects on each other, a distinctive travel culture is created by a variety of actors and information is spread using various forms of information technology, which in turn attracts more people with similar interests.

Otaku tourism involves meetings in real spaces of various people of diverse interests who have engaged in the collection and dissemination of information. In sites of otaku tourism, connections are created between people whom we would not normally expect to come together. Otaku tourists, by pursuing their interests to the limits and embarking on journeys to visit sites related to the contents they enjoy, have chance encounters with others. Through those encounters and a desire to enjoy the travel experience, they have ended up creating new forms of communication both among fans themselves and also between the fans and local people in those communities that host anime sacred sites.

Notes

1. Azuma Hiroki's seminal 2001 book *Dōbutsuka suru posutomodan* was translated into English in 2009. Citations from this book are taken from the 2009 English version. When Azuma's work is referred to in other Japanese language sources, the 2001 version is cited.
2. Other definitions focus on forms of behaviour, clothing or communication styles. See, for example, Tagawa (2009, pp. 73–80) and Yoshimoto (2009).
3. As Nakajima (1991) argues, there are a number of significant differences between *dōjinshi* produced by men and women. In this article, otaku refers mainly to males and I am analysing their anime pilgrimage. Female anime pilgrimage is a topic for further research, although the related topic of travel by *rekijo* (female history fans) is the subject of the article by Sugawa-Shimada Akiko in this issue. For more information on fan-produced magazines by and for women, see Kaneda (2007).
4. Imai (2009, 2010) and Sato (2010) analyse anime pilgrimage from a religious perspective.
5. Database Top Page: http://www.so-net.ne.jp/database/G-search/general/general_ohdan.html
6. For an online example of a fan's pilgrimage, see http://www7.atpages.jp/sasa90/seichi-rakisuta.html [Accessed 5 June 2014].
7. For an example of a fan's site that compares scenes from the anime with actual locations, see http://seesaawiki.jp/w/lsh_er/d/TV%A5%A2%A5%CB%A5%E1%A1%D8%CE%C3%B5%DC%A5%CF%A5%EB%A5%D2%A4%CE%CD%AB%DD%B5%A1%D9%C9%F1%C2%E6%C3%B5%CB%AC%A4%DE%A4%C8%A4%E1%A5%B5%A5%A4%A5%C8 [Accessed 5 June 2014].
8. This can be seen at http://www.youtube.com/watch?v=iWtbU7_KDFs&feature=related [Accessed 2 June 2014].
9. For an example of a fan's site that compares scenes from the anime and actual locations, see <http://seesaawiki.jp/w/lsh_er/d/%A4%B1%A4%A4%A4%AA%A4%F3%A1%AA%C9%F1%C2%E6%C3%B5%CB%AC/%C0%BB%C3%CF%BD%E4%CE%E9%40%B5%EC%CB%AD%B6%BF%BE%AE%B3%D8%B9%BB%237%A1%C1%2313 [Accessed 5 June 2014].

References

Azuma, H., 2001. *Dōbutsuka suru posutomodan: otaku kara mita nihon shakai*. Tokyo: Kōdansha Gendai Shinsho.

Azuma, H., 2009. *Otaku: Japan's database animals*, trans. J. E Able and S. Kono. Minneapolis: University of Minnesota Press.

Drill Project, 2010. *Anime & komikku, seichi junrei navi.* Tokyo: Asuka shinsha.

Endo, H., 2010. Kankō no kairaku wo meguru 'gaibu no yuibutsuron': 'asobi' = 'tawamure' wo jiku to shita shakai kōsō. *In:* H. Endo and M. Horino, eds. *Kankō Shakaigaku no akuchuariti.* Kyoto: Kōyō Shobō, 22–39.

Fujiyama, T., 2006. *Moeru seichi Akiba ritānzu: Akihabara maniakkusu 2006.* Tokyo: Mainichi komyunikēshonzu.

Giddens, A., 1991. *Modernity and self-identity: self and society in the late modern age.* Palo Alto, CA: Stanford University Press.

Hasegawa, F. and Midorikawa, K., 2005. *Kontentsu bijinesu ga chiiki wo kaeru.* Tokyo: NTT Shuppan.

Hashimoto, H., 2006. Matsuri: tsukurareru tabi. *In:* T. Oguchi, ed. *Kankō no shakai shinrigaku: hito koto mono mittsu no shiten kara.* Kyoto: Kitaōji Shobō, 167–183.

Imai, N., 2009. Anime 'seichi junrei' jissensha no kōdō ni miru dentōteki junrei to kankō katsudō no kakyō kanōsei: Saitama-ken Washimiya jinja hōnō ema bunseki o chūshin ni. *CATS sōsho*, 1, 87–111.

Imai, N., 2010. Kontentsu ga motarasu basho kaishaku no henyō: Saitama-ken Washimiya jinja hōnō ema hikaku bunseki o chūshin ni. *Kontentsu bunkashi kenkyū*, 3, 69–86.

Japan Travel and Tourism Association, 2010. *Heisei 22-nendo ban, kankō no jittai to shikō.* Tokyo: JTTA.

JTB Publishing, 2008. *Moe rurubu Cool Japan otaku Nippon gaido.* Tokyo: JTB Publishing.

Kakizaki, S., 2005. *Seichi junrei: anime, manga 12-kasho meguri.* Tokyo: Kirutaimu komyunikēshon.

Kanda, K., 2012. Shirakawa-gō e no anime seichi junrei to chiiki no hannō: basho imēji oyobi kankōkyaku wo meguru bunka seiji. *Kankōgaku*, 7, 23–28.

Kaneda, J., 2007. Manga dōjinshi: kaishaku kyōdōtai no poritikusu. *In:* K. Satō and S. Yoshimi, eds. *Bunka no shakaigaku.* Tokyo: Yūhikaku, 163–190.

Kobayashi, Y., 1999. Terebi, anime no media fandamu: majokko anime no sekai. *In:* M. Itō and S. Fujita, eds. *Terebijon, porifonī: bangumi, shichōsha bunseki no kokoromi.* Kyoto: Sekai shisōsha, 182–215.

Lyotard, J., 1979. *La Condition postmoderne*, trans. Y. Kobayashi, 1989. *Posutomodan no jōken: chi, shakai, gengo.* Tokyo: Suiseisha.

Masubuchi, T., 2010. *Monogatari wo tabi suru hitobito: kontentsu tsūrizumu to wa nani ka*, Tokyo: Sairyūsha.

Ministry of Internal Affairs and Communications, 2005. u-Japan Policy homepage. Available from: http://www.soumu.go.jp/menu_seisaku/ict/u-japan_en/index.html [Accessed 2 June 2014].

Ministry of Internal Affairs and Communications, 2011. Heisei 23-nendoban jōhō tsūshin hakusho: kyōseigata netto shakai no jitsugen ni mukete. Tokyo: Ministry of Internal Affairs and Communications.

Murase, H., 2003. Otaku to iu ōdiensu. *In:* N Kobayashi and Y. Mōri, eds. *Terebi wa dō mirarete kita no ka.* Tokyo: Serika Shobō, 133–152.

Nakajima, A., 1991. *Komyunikēshon fuzen shōkōgun.* Tokyo: Chikuma Shobō.

Namba, K., 2007. *Zoku no keifugaku: yūsu-sabukaruchāzu no sengoshi.* Tokyo: Seikyūsha.

Okamoto, T., 2008. Anime seichi ni okeru junreisha no dōkō haaku hōhō no kentō: seichi junrei nōto bunseki no yūkōsei to kadai ni tsuite. *Kankō sōzō kenkyū*, 2, 1–13. Available from: http://hdl.handle.net/2115/34672 [Accessed 2 June 2014].

Okamoto, T., 2010. Gendai Nihon ni okeru wakamono no tabi bunka ni kansuru kenkyū: anime seichi junrei wo jirei to shite. *Tabi no bunka kenkyūjo kenkyū hōkoku*, 19, 1–19.

Okamoto, T., 2013. *n-ji sōsaku kankō: anime seichi junrei / kontentsu tsūrizumu / kankō shakaigaku no kanōsei.* Ebetsu: Hokkaidō Bōken Geijutsu Shuppan.

Osawa, M., 2008. *Fukanōsei no jidai*. Tokyo: Iwanami Shoten.

Roesch, S., 2009. *The experiences of film location tourists*. Bristol: Channel View.

Saitama Shinbun, 2011. Seichi ni wakamono monogatari taikan. *Saitama Shinbun*, 31 December, p. 19.

Sato, Y., 2010. Otaku ema to wa nani ka: Miyagi-ken gokoku jinja no ema chōsa kekka to sono bunseki. *CATS sōsho*, 4, 115–127 .

Tagami, H., 2007. *Dejitaru komyunikēshon: ICT no kiso chishiki*. Kyoto: Kōyō Shobō.

Tagawa, T., 2009. Otaku bunseki no hōkōsei. *Nagoya Bunri Daigaku Kiyō*, 9, 73–80.

Tomita, H., 2009. *Intimeito sutorenjā: 'tokumeisei' to 'shinmitsusei' wo meguru bunka shakaigakuteki kenkyū*. Osaka: Kansai Daigaku Shuppanbu.

Uno, T., 2008. *Zero nendai no sōzōryoku*. Tokyo: Hayakawa Shobō.

Yamada, Y., 2008. Tasha to deau: shihai no yokkyū kara deai no yokkyu e no tenkai. *In:* S. Ishimori, ed. *Daikōryū jidai ni okeru kankō sōzō*. Sapporo: Hokkaido daigaku daigakuin media komyunikēshon kenkyūin sōsho 70, 249–266.

Yamada, Y., 2009. Manazashi wo okuru: posuto kyokō no jidai ni okeru tasha to no deai (zenpen). *The Northern Review*, 36, 17–30.

Yamada, Y., 2011. Manazashi wo okuru: posuto kyokō no jidai ni okeru tasha to no deai (kōhen). *The Northern Review*, 37, 11–45.

Yamamura, T., 2011. *Anime, Manga de chiiki shinkō: machi no fan wo umu kontentsu tsūrizumu kaihatsuhō*. Tokyo: Tokyo Hōrei Shuppan.

Yoshida, J., 2008. Kankō sōzō no hōhō to hōkō: neotsūrizumu to bunka dezain. *In:* S. Ishimori, ed. *Daikōryū jidai ni okeru kankō sōzō*. Sapporo: Hokkaido daigaku daigakuin media komyunikēshon kenkyūin sōsho 70, 229–248.

Yoshimoto, T., 2009. *Otaku no kigen*, Tokyo: NTT Shuppan.

Takeshi Okamoto is a lecturer in the Faculty of Regional Promotion, Nara Prefectural University. He completed his PhD in tourism studies at Hokkaido University in 2012. His research focuses on tourism, popular culture and communication theory. He is the co-author (with Yamamura Takayoshi) of *Current issues in contents tourism: aspects of tourism in an information-based society* (CATS Library Vol. 7) and *n-th creation tourism: anime pilgrimage, contents tourism and the sociology of tourism* published by Hokkaido Bōken Geijutsu Shuppan (both in Japanese).

Rekijo, pilgrimage and 'pop-spiritualism': pop-culture-induced heritage tourism of/for young women

AKIKO SUGAWA-SHIMADA

Abstract: Since around 2008, a new type of eager consumption of Japanese traditional, cultural and ideological images and notions has been exhibited by young women in Japan. Called *rekijo* (history fan girls), they have attracted great public attention. They enjoy visiting historical sites that appear in anime, novels and videogames based on historical fact, and actively participate in events led by local communities. The popularity of such 'contents tourism' or 'pilgrimage' has had a significant economic effect. Simultaneously, a 'power spot' boom has taken place, in which young women visit Shinto shrines, Buddhist temples and historical sites to gain spiritual power. Their '"pop" nationalistic' faith towards the spirits of historical figures, Shinto *kami* and Buddha may be called 'pop-spiritualism' and contributes to building new notions of 'Japanese-ness'. This article explores the significance of the heritage tourism of young women in socio-cultural and feminist contexts, and discusses how the recent *rekijo* phenomenon and women's 'pop-spiritualism' serves to reconceptualize their national identities and challenge Japanese gender norms. These processes are exemplified through discussion of women's heritage tourism induced by *An-an* and *Non-no* in the 1970s, historical dramas in the 1980s, the *Mirage of Blaze* series in the 1990s and *Sengoku BASARA* and *Hakuōki* in the 2000s.

The *rekijo* phenomenon

Recently, some young Japanese women have adopted Japanese traditional, cultural and ideological images and notions that were traditionally the domain of older men. They are called *rekijo*, or 'history fan girls', and are young women (*joshi*) who embrace Japanese history (*rekishi*). The term *rekijo* was inspired by the term *rekidoru* (*rekishi aidoru*, or young female idols and models who love history), which was coined in 2008 when the film *Red cliff* was released in Japan.

Red cliff, based on the Chinese historical text *The records of three kingdoms* (*Sango-kushi*), was promoted by *rekidoru* such as Kohinata Eri, Mikako and An (Fuka-zawa 2009). History, which was seen mainly as an (elderly) male interest, became positively associated with young women. The term *rekijo* first appeared in the Japanese press in the *Asahi shinbun* on 30 March 2009. Since then, media discourses on *rekijo* have multiplied and '*rekijo*' was chosen as one of the phrases of the year in 2009. The *rekijo* phenomenon has become a 'fashionable' trend among young women.

Another form of this interest in history among young women is the so-called 'power spot' boom, the term given to visits by young women to Shinto shrines, temples and spiritual places connected with historical events or legends to gain spiritual power. *CREA*, a women's magazine targeting young working women, ran a feature 'Power spots all over Japan' in 2010, inducing many female tourists to visit shrines, temples and sites related to spiritual energy (Anon 2010).

Then there are *butsuzō gyaru* or *butsujo*, young women who revere statues of Buddha. They also attracted public interest when numerous young women were noticed appreciating statues of Buddha at temples and exhibitions.

These phenomena are precipitating visible changes within Japanese society. With more young women visiting Buddhist temples to view the statues, more women are now in the audiences of Buddhist monks' sermons in the temples (Hamana 2009). In 2009 'The National Treasure *Ashura* and Masterpieces from Kofukuji' exhibition at Tokyo National Museum (part of the 1300th anniversary of Nara becoming the capital of Japan) had approximately 15,000 visitors per day, the largest average visitors-per-day among all art exhibitions in the world that year (*The Art Newspaper* 2010, p. 23). Many young female visitors saw the statues not as 'depressing' but as 'adorable and healing' and this change in perception among young women towards Buddhism contributed to the success of the exhibition (Shinada 2009, p. 7). In the same year, 8.6 million people visited Ise Jingu Shrine in Mie Prefecture, which is the central Shinto shrine that worships the sun goddess Amaterasu-ōmikami. This was a record for annual visitors to the shrine since 1945 (*Asahi shinbun* 2010b). One reason for the increase in visitors was that more young visitors, especially females, came in search of connection with the spiritual power of the gods, *kami*, at Shinto shrines.[1]

In this socio-cultural context, *rekijo* represent a gender-crossover phenomenon between largely segregated domains based on gender differences in Japan. The phenomenon was 'discovered' in the early 2000s, partly because the Basic Law for a Gender-Equal Society enacted in 1999 promoted a notion of gender equality among young people. Changes in the formerly gender-biased school curriculums and campaigns for gender equality have gradually instilled an understanding of gender equality at schools and workplaces (Cabinet Office 2009). This has facilitated a re-conceptualization of gender images. Therefore, women no longer hesitate to enter male-dominated entertainment fields related to Japanese history. On the other hand, there has also been a backlash against gender equality in which a growing number of young women have stated a prefer- ence for becoming a 'housewife' (Shirakawa 2009). This may be attributed in part to a loss in enthusiasm among women for job-hunting caused by lower female employment rates in all age brackets for full-time jobs (Ministry of Health, Labour and Welfare 2010, p. 62). However, it also represents a form of nostalgia and a desire to re-value 'Japanese tradition' that has been lost (Suzuki 2009, p. 20). Thus the traditional forms of masculinity represented by Ashura or male characters in pop-cultural products fascinate many *rekijo*.

Another reason for the growing phenomenon of *rekijo* may be new marketing strategies that have contributed to the breakdown of gender segregation. Since the bursting of the economic bubble in the early 1990s, women have been tar- geted in marketing strategies and used in advertisements to attract female con- sumers to male-dominated interests, for instance, horse racing and gambling. They are considered potential customers in the field of heritage tourism as well. For instance, the Utsunomiya Secret Tour, in which tourists traced the places related to Hijikata Toshizō (a member of the Shinsengumi, the shogunal guard unit that assassinated anti-shogunal forces in Kyoto between 1863 and 1867) in Utsunomiya, Tochigi, was planned primarily to appeal to *rekijo* (*Asahi shinbun* 2010a, Arase 2011, pp. 3–4). In another example, the Shiga prefectural govern- ment collaborated with JTB, the largest tourist agency in Japan, and recruited *rekijo* bloggers to promote tourism to Shiga during the tourism promotion cam- paigns that coincided with the 2011 NHK Taiga drama, *Go* (Kensei e-shinbun 2010). Similarly, following the popularity of the videogame and anime *Sengoku BASARA*, JTB offered history tours entitled 'Visiting historical places related to Sengoku samurai warriors' in Tohoku, Shinshū, Jōetsu, Sekigahara, Chūgoku and Shikoku between October 2010 and March 2011 (JTB 2010). Female par- ticipants comprised 90 per cent of the total (Oricon life 2009). The estimated annual economic effect of *rekijo* was seventy billion yen, covering tourism and merchandizing (Fuji Film 2010; see also the article by Philip Seaton in this issue). The *rekijo*'s economic effect was demonstrated by the success of anime- related products in Miyagi, such as BASARA rice and BASARA beer (Nakano 2009). In a manner similar to the way that male-fan contents tourism induced by anime has contributed to the successful revitalization of local economies and communities (see the articles by Okamoto Takeshi and Yamamura Takayoshi in this issue), *rekijo*'s heritage tourism has attracted much attention for the potential business opportunities that it offers.

The *rekijo* phenomenon, therefore, has had a broad impact in areas such as gender equality, perspectives on Japanese history, spiritualism, the economy and societal change in Japan.

Women's heritage tourism induced by pop culture

Becoming a *rekijo* is a new trend among young women that started in the 2000s. Numerous women became *rekijo* as a result of the videogame/anime *Sengoku*

BASARA (based on the history of the Warring States Period during the late fifteenth and late sixteenth centuries), the girls' videogame/anime *Hakuōki,* and the manga/anime *Gintama* (the latter two were based on the history of the Bakumatsu Period, 1853–1868, particularly the shogunal guard unit Shinsengumi). In Japan the term 'pilgrimage' (*seichi junrei*) is used to denote visits by fans of audio-visual culture to the locations where those audio-visual works are set. Such pop-culture-mediated pilgrimage to sites that are related to historical events has been actively conducted by *rekijo*, resulting in changes to the demographics of heritage tourism. In Japan today, popular periods of Japanese history such as the Warring States and Bakumatsu periods are routinely represented in popular cultural forms such as manga, anime, TV dramas and films. Consuming history is often equivalent to consuming pop-cultural products.

The recent emergence of the *rekijo* phenomenon might give the impression that young women have suddenly grown more religious or conservative, as shown by increased female interest in Japanese history and sacred sites. However, similar phenomena were observed in the 1970s when many young women visited 'unknown shrines and temples' after reading feature articles about those sites in the women's fashion magazines *An-an* and *Non-no*. In the 1980s, when TV dramas such as the NHK Taiga drama and NTV's (Nippon Television Network) year-end special period dramas cast handsome young actors as famous historical figures, young women visited the protagonists' tombs and historical sites. Then in the 1990s, *Mirage of blaze,* a girls' novel series which depicts Uesugi Kagetora from the Sengoku Period, triggered the 'mirage tour' (visiting protagonists' tombs, shrines and temples and sites connected to the story) by female fans, called *mirajennu* (Hashimoto 2006, p. 178).[2] In a manner similar to the *rekijo* phenomenon, these phenomena were induced by the mass media. However, they may also have stemmed from young women's nostalgic appreciation and reconceptualization of 'Japanese-ness'. Especially since the late 1990s, their '"pop" nationalistic' faith towards Shinto's *kami,* Buddha and even dead sprits – a phenomenon I call 'pop-spiritualism' – has contributed to the revision of notions of 'Japanese-ness'.

Although young women who are fans of Japanese history and visit 'power spots' are not uncommon, why does the *rekijo* phenomenon attract so much current public interest? If *rekijo* may exist anytime and anywhere, how does the *rekijo* phenomenon that emerged in the 2000s differ from female history fans in other decades? And, if the *rekijo* phenomenon is effectively a version of 'anime pilgrimage' or pop culture tourism, how does it differ from broader anime-induced and male (otaku) contents tourism?

In order to answer these questions, this article first explores how young women were used as agents to reconstruct nostalgic notions of 'traditional Japan' and how they used 'Japanese-ness' in seeking psychological safe havens in the 1970s–1980s. It then argues that women's contents tourism related to history in the 1990s and the 2000s differs from men's contents tourism in the context of 'pop-spiritualism' by analysing women's pilgrimages induced by the *Mirage of blaze* series (1990–2004), the *Sengoku BASARA* series (videogame 2005–, anime 2009–2010, Film 2011, TV drama 2012) and the *Hakuōki* series (videogame 2008–, anime 2010, 2012, 2014).

The *An-Non* Tribe and 'Discover Japan' campaign in the 1970s

Prior to the 1970s, female solo tourists were often unwelcome at inns or lodges because women without male companions or their families were seen as troublesome, or having 'an unusual reason' for travelling alone, such as having been jilted and thereby possibly searching for a place to attempt suicide. However, in the 1970s, women were 'visualized' as potential customers in the context of women's liberation movements. A new type of women's fashion magazine, exemplified by *An-an* and *Non-no* (first published in 1970 and 1971, respectively), featured women travelling around Japan (Akagi 2007, pp. 193–194). This created a surge in the popularity of solo women's travel all over Japan to 'discover Japanese-ness' (Saitō 2001 [2000], p. 235), such as tranquillity in Shinto shrines, Buddhist temples and Japanese gardens, and little-known Japanese traditional dishes and sweets. Often travelling with their copy of *An-an* and/or *Non-no*, these women were called the 'An-Non Tribe', and came to represent a fashionable style of women's tourism (Hayashi 2005, p. 3; Masubuchi 2010, pp. 39–40). In 1978, Japan National Railway (now Japan Railway) started a 'Discover Japan' campaign, using young women in fashionable clothing in its TV advertisement 'Discover Japan and re-discover your (true) self'. The campaign also featured an up-and-coming pop singer, Yamaguchi Momoe. Her campaign song *A good day, departure (Iihi tabidachi)*, portraying a solo female tourist, was an instant success and increased the numbers of female customers taking train journeys (Hayashi 2005, pp. 2–3; Masubuchi 2010, p. 40).

In the 1970s, there were drastic changes in young women's lives, such as an increasing proportion of women receiving higher education,[3] longer periods of employment and the delay of marriage (Sakamoto 1999). A growing number of young working women could afford to rent their own flats in urban areas. *An-an* and *Non-no* featured not only women's travel but also interior designs to encourage them to have their own homes. Therefore, while prejudice against solo female travellers remained, the *An-Non* Tribe and the growing social mobility of women challenged the notion that women were supposed to be socially invisible. Young women's tourism thus served not only to emphasize their financial and psychological independence, but also to destabilize gender norms.

Drama-induced heritage tourism in the 1980s

In the 1980s, the number of female history fans increased when heartthrob actors were cast in popular films and television dramas. For instance, NHK's Taiga drama *Tōge no Gunzō* (1982), based on the famous 'Forty-seven Ronin' story (*Chūshingura*), cast top idol singer Go Hiromi as Kataoka Gengoemon, one of the forty-seven masterless samurai of the ex-Akō clan who committed suicide (*seppuku*) after avenging the death of their feudal lord. After Kataoka died in the drama, it was reported that young women rushed into his tomb and prayed at the Loyalist Festival in Sengakuji Temple in Tokyo (*Yomiuri shinbun* 1982a, 1982b).

Another example is Okita Sōji, one of the most popular historical figures among young women. He was a young warrior in the Shinsengumi. Okita was one of the strongest warriors but died young of tuberculosis. His role has been played by handsome up-and-coming actors in many films and TV dramas since the 1960s. For instance, Shimada Junshi was cast in *Shinsengumi keppū roku* (1965) and *Moeyo ken* (1970), which were adapted from Shiba Ryōtarō's bestselling novels of the same titles. Kusakari Masao, a half-American half-Japanese actor, played the titular character of the film *Okita Sōshi* (1974).[4] Their performances of Okita portrayed a sympathetic young man who was tragically involved in the chaos of the Bakumatsu (1853–1868) period. On New Year's Eve between 1985 and 1993, the NTV network broadcast a special period drama, which frequently depicted the Bakumatsu period.[5] The role of Okita Sōji in *Byakko tai* (1986) and *Kihei tai* (1989) was played by Nakagawa Katsuhiko, a handsome and popular rock singer, whose female fans followed him from the music world to historical dramas. His Okita was a nihilistic and beautiful killer. The setting of *Byakko tai*, Aizu-Wakamatsu in Fukushima, saw an increase in visitors, also inspired in part by the hit theme song, *Lovable days* (*Itoshiki hibi*), by Horiuchi Takao.

The popularity of Okita has continued to the present day. In the 1990s, *Shinsengumi keppū roku* (1998) was remade with Nakamura Shunsuke, a popular idol/actor, cast as Okita. As Nakamura's first role in a period drama, it attracted great media attention. In the 2000s, NHK's Taiga drama *Shinsengumi!* (2004) had the handsome and talented actor Fujiwara Tatsuya in the role of Okita. His portrayal was of a naive and humane young boy who was strong but afraid of dying. Okita as a nihilistic killer reappeared in the *Hakuōki* series (2010), the TV anime based on the mega-hit video game for girls of the same title, and *Gintama* (2006–2010, 2011–2012) adapted from Sorachi Hideaki's manga of the same title. Both these series have induced pilgrimage to Mibu Temple in Kyoto and other sites related to Shinsengumi too (which will be revisited later).

Tourism induced by *Mirage of blaze* in the 1990s–2000s

The so-called 'mirage tour', tourism by women induced by the *Mirage of blaze* series, is probably the beginning of women's heritage tourism induced by pop culture and the first example which can be categorized as contemporary contents tourism (Iwai 2009, p. 47). The *Mirage of blaze* series is Kuwabara Mizuna's psychic action fantasy for young readers (or 'light novel').[6] Based on historical fact, it is about Uesugi Kagetora (the first adopted son of Uesugi Kenshin) who lost a war over who would succeed his father with Uesugi Kagekatsu (the second adopted son of Kenshin). It is set after the two men's stepfather's death in Echigo (Niigata) in the Sengoku Period. The story is set in 1990. A high school boy, Ōgi Takaya, is told that he is Uesugi Kagetora by Naoe Nobutsuna, who was his former enemy 400 years ago, but has been reborn to be his mentor and subordinate. Although Takaya/Kagetora has lost his memory, their souls continue living by borrowing others' bodies for 400 years. A number of vengeful spirits of 'losers' in Japanese history, including Oda Nobunaga, start taking vengeance called 'Dark Sengoku'. They possess and hurt living people. Kagetora and Naoe and three other followers of Uesugi, nicknamed the *yasha-shū* (demons) of the Uesugi, fight against the vengeful spirits to subdue them with their esoteric Buddhist power. Thus, historical facts, *goryō shinkō* (the folk religious belief in vengeful sprits) and spiritualism of esoteric Buddhism are combined in the plot of *Mirage of blaze*.

The *Mirage of blaze* series was adapted into multiple media formats, including CD dramas (1992–1997), manga (2001), TV anime series (2002) and original animation video (OVA) (2004), as part of a 'mixed-media' marketing strategy. This series proved instantly popular among teenage girls and young women who began the 'mirage tour': visits to sites related to Kagetora and Naoe, such as Uesugi Shrine and the Uesugi Festival in Yonezawa, Yamagata, the ruins of Samegao Castle in Niigata (where it is said Uesugi Kagetora killed himself in 1579 aged 26) and other locations in the story across the country.

In 2008, approximately fifty women (dubbed *mirajennu*) participated in the 429th memorial ceremony for Kagetora at Shōfukuji Temple near the ruins of the castle (*Asahi shinbun* 2008), which was unusual for a memorial ceremony for a little-known historical figure. At the Uesugi Festival, the well-known Battle of Kawanakajima (1561) between Uesugi Kenshin and Takeda Shingen is re-enacted by local people in period costumes. The re-enactments include historical figures that appear in or are connected to *Mirage of blaze*. The conspicuous presence of *mirajennu* at these events is indicated by a comment in Kuwabara's postscript to volume 8 of the novel: 'I was nervous about a demographic change at the Uesugi Festival this year. There were some groups of girls who were extremely excited [about the Battle]. Well, dear readers, please try not to bother others, OK?' (Kuwabara 1992, p. 242).

From this we can conclude that the mirage tour phenomenon had already begun by 1992. The female fans photographed those who played the roles of historical figures related to the novel, such as Irobe Katsunaga and Yasuda Nagahide. The growing numbers of *mirajennu* visiting the Uesugi Festival had an impact on local communities in Yonezawa. For instance, due to the great popularity of Naoe Nobutsuna in *Mirage of blaze*, a new unit led by Naoe Kagetsuna (Nobutsuna's father) was set up for the re-enactment of the Battle of Kawanakajima at the Uesugi Festival, which was clearly intended to appeal to *mirajennu* (Kuwabara 1994, p. 255), and a bottle of rosé wine named 'Chigiri' (noose) was produced as a souvenir for *mirajennu* by a local brewer in collaboration with female students of a local college (Hashimoto 2006, p. 179; *Asahi shinbun* 1997). These are early examples of contents tourism influencing local culture, business and communication dynamics (see also the article by Yamamura Takayoshi in this issue).

However, the particular characteristic of the mirage tour differs from the broader category of contemporary contents tourism in that the focus is not only on narratives or narrative quality (*monogatarisei*) but also on the relationships/connections (*kankeisei*) between fictional characters, readers and actual historical figures. The great popularity of the mirage tour can be understood in terms of the multi-layered relationships between these three actors. On the level of fantasy, *mirajennu* appreciate relationships between the characters (for example, Takaya and Naoe) in the story, and enjoy coupling characters (for example, Naoe and Kōsaka, Naoe's opponent) in the manner of a boys' love (BL)[7] story or relating *mirajennu* to their favourite characters (for example, Naoe and 'I'). Then they visualize their invented stories in the form of their creative products, for example *dōjinshi* (self-published novels and manga). On the level of reality, *mirajennu* conduct mirage tours in search of psychological connections to the protagonists/historical figures and even their dead souls, which also act to draw fantasy worlds into the real one (a point which will be discussed further below).

In order to strengthen readers' relationships (*kankeisei*) to the characters, an attractive storyline is crucial. In fact, *Mirage of blaze* contains serious social issues relevant to young women in the 1990s: abandoned children, lost identity, apathy towards life and the difficulties of romance. Takaya experiences his alcoholic father's domestic violence, his parents' divorce and his teachers' oppression against him in school in 1990s Japan. In the story Kagetora was raped by his elder brother's subordinates during his childhood in his hometown, Sagami (Kanagawa), and was betrayed by his stepbrother and subordinates in Echigo 400 years ago. As a result of these traumas he is still unable to trust people. This allows readers with similar problems to associate with him. Takaya's consistent soulsearching about the meanings of life, in particular, appealed to those going through the instabilities of adolescence. Takaya, who has lost his memory about his previous lives, accuses Naoe of possessing others' bodies and having eternal life. However, after his first encounter with vengeful spirits, Takaya speaks to Naoe as follows:

'I somehow understood what you said, "Dead souls are the same as us." They lived in the past, but they were humans like us.' 'Yes,' said Naoe calmly. 'So we must not be arrogant just because we are alive now. I believe that we should respect them as human beings, too.'

(Kuwabara 2005 [1992], p. 236)

Realizing that he is also a vengeful spirit, Takaya (Kagetora) is worn out by his guilty conscience for having snatched his body from the soul of another. In the second half of the series, Takaya, who has to face the end of his soul, exhorts living people on TV that they should live their lives so that they never become vengeful spirits full of regrets and grudges. This sentiment might have enabled *mirajennu* to empathize with the fictional characters and to nurture a respectful attitude towards dead souls.

In reality, from 1990 to the early 2000s, Japanese society experienced serious political, economic and social instabilities caused by the Great Hanshin Earthquake and the Aum Shinrikyo cult's sarin gas attack on the Tokyo subway in 1995, and by the aftermath of the bubble economy. Particularly those who were in their 20s during the 1990s feared Nostradamus' prophesy about 'the end of the world in 1999' (Inoue 1999, pp. 60–62, 68). Concomitant with an emerging occult boom in the 1970s, Nostradamus' prophesy became a craze among children in the 1970s, stirred up by Gotō Ben's best-seller *Nostradamus' predictions* (1973) and a film of the same title (1974). In the book/film, a sixteenth-century French physician/astrologist Michel de Nostredame (Nostradamus) predicted catastrophe in his poetry, which suggested that the king of fear would descend to the earth in 1999. This apocalyptic vision was sensationally reported on TV and visualized in the film, imprinting potential fear about the end of the world in 1999 in the minds of children growing up in the 1970s. Fears were stoked again by a number of manga published in 1999: for instance, Sakura Momoko's *Chibi Maruko-chan* (1986–1996), Ishigaki Yuki's *MMR* (1991–1999), Takaya Natsuki's *Fruits basket* (1998–2006) and Takahashi Shin's *Saishū heiki kanojo* (*She: the ultimate weapon*) (2000–2001). In this context of social instability and anxiety, the meanings of life and death that *Mirage of blaze* addresses appealed to young female readers.

Furthermore, the relationship between Takaya and Naoe fascinates *mirajennu*. For 400 years, Naoe has been jealous of Kagetora's intelligence and absolute power. Naoe has admired Kagetora, but simultaneously hated him, and eventually admitted his love for him. Kagetora/Takaya, however, is unable to return this love as he fears trusting people, so he continuously refuses Naoe's advances even though he desperately desires him. Their complicated love-hate relationship ultimately ends in mutual eternal commitment. The boys' love storyline in *Mirage of blaze* was one of the most important factors prompting *mirajennu* to conduct their mirage tours. Some cases were reported where *mirajennu* visited shrines to dedicate *ema* (wooden plaques at Shinto shrines on which people write their wishes), wishing for the happiness of the characters (Henshūbu 1998, p. 87; Kuwabara 1993, pp. 266–267). *Mirajennu* who conducted mirage tours often wrote in their blogs, 'I will go and meet Takaya and Naoe' (Mirage tour community 2012). These *mirajennu* obviously see Takaya and Naoe as a couple and seek connections between Takaya and Naoe and themselves.

Such relationship-oriented tourism by women can be explained by women's desire to connect with others. Psychoanalyst Saitō Tamaki suggests that:

> Men are never at ease unless they possess a social 'position'. This can be attributed to men's desire for possession. However, women do not demand social positions in the way that men do. Women tend to maintain their identities through their 'relationships' with others.

(Saitō 2009, p. 118)

Additionally, referring to the work of Enomoto Nariko, Saitō analyses female BL fans in terms of their attention to relationships:

> Female BL fans demonstrate longing (*moe*) for '*isō*', according to Enomoto. *Isō* signifies hierarchical relationships. Let us suppose that friendship and conflicts between boys are depicted in boys' manga. What female BL fans will be strongly attracted to are the relationships themselves.

(Saitō 2009, p. 151)

Although Saitō's analysis is not necessarily applicable to all women and might be interpreted as essentialist, his remarks on women's enthusiasm for relationships or connections mirrors *mirajennu*'s motivations in going on mirage tours to build connections between characters, between characters and readers, and between readers and historical figures via characters.

The mirage tour also gained popularity via media coverage as well. Guidebooks edited by Shūeisha, the publisher of *Mirage of blaze*, introduced the actual locations in the story with detailed maps, photos and extracts from the novel (Henshūbu 1998; Kuwabara 2001). Author Kuwabara's own travel experiences were also published in 1994. In the 2000s, social network services (SNS) and individuals' blogs enabled *mirajennu* to describe their experiences of their own mirage tours and share photos, thereby allowing them to interact with other *mirajennu*. On mixi, the largest SNS in Japan, in June 2012 there were seven communities related to *Mirage of blaze*, the largest of which had 2,041 registered members. Another 420 users were registered in a community for those who had taken the mirage tour.

Heritage tourism induced by *Sengoku BASARA* and *Hakuōki* in the 2000s

In the 2000s, many women became *rekijo* as a result of *Sengoku BASARA* and *Hakuōki*, whose contents appeared in many different media forms. The anime series of *Sengoku BASARA* (2009–2010) was adapted from Capcom's action videogame series of the same title, which was first released in 2005. Although based on historical fact and set in the Sengoku period, the protagonists are fashionably and uniquely characterized, which was appealing to *rekijo* (Iwai 2009, p.

48). For instance, Date Masamune speaks English and Sanada Yukimura is a hyper-vigorous, warm-hearted young man. Some female warriors are also featured, although they are in the minority.

Similarly, *Hakuōki* is a romance adventure videogame produced by Idea Factory aimed at women and featuring various handsome young men based on actual key members of the Shinsengumi, including Hijikata Toshizō, Okita Sōji and Tōdō Heisuke. It was adapted into an anime series (2010, 2012), prompting female fans to conduct pilgrimages to Kyoto, Tokyo and Hokkaido.

The popularity of these works among women can be attributed to several factors: (1) easy gameplay through simplified game console controls (women tend to be reluctant to operate complicated controls: *Asahi shinbun* 2009b, Nakamura 2009), (2) a growing number of cosplay (dressing up as favourite characters) events held all over Japan where *rekijo* could perform their favourite characters, (3) diverse male characters that *rekijo* would take pleasure in coupling together in the BL context ('team *danshi moe*') and (4) attractive secondary characters portrayed as young sympathetic men with tragic ends, who are historically considered rebels and losers (Sakai 2008). Here, the final two factors are particularly relevant to the discussion of *rekijo*'s heritage tourism.

'History' tends to highlight the lives of men discursively. Although female characters are featured in the anime *Sengoku BASARA* and *Hakuōki*, they are almost always marginalized from the main storyline (such as Kichō and Ichi in *Sengoku BASARA*) or serve to support male homosocial bonds (such as Chizuru in *Hakuōki*). This enables female fans to be outsiders gazing at men in an all-male environment without identifying themselves with female characters. This is called 'team *danshi moe* (enthusiasm/affection for a boys' team)' (Kawaguchi 2010). The variety in types of male characters (such as the big brother type, younger brother type, intelligent type and macho type) stimulates *rekijo*'s creative imaginations: they take pleasure not only in coupling fictional characters but also constructing virtual relationships between their favourite characters and themselves. The interplay between the real and the virtual are embodied in heritage tourism.

For instance, Figures 1, 2 and 3 are extracts from visitors' notebooks kept in Mibuzuka (where there are the graves of ten Shinsengumi members and other memorials) in Mibu temple in Kyoto, where the Mibu rōshigumi (later renamed Shinsengumi) was first stationed. The illustration in Figure 1 is the character of Tōdō Heisuke in *Hakuōki*, indicating that this fan's affection for Heisuke motivated her to visit the temple. The writer in Figure 2, Yui, says: 'I love OKITA SŌJI. Don't let tuberculosis beat you! I really love the contrast: you're a great swordsman but weak and sick. Just kill me.' Her writings suggest her intimacy with the historical figure through representations of Okita, probably in anime. Figure 3 shows Okita in *Hakuōki*, indicating the visitor's love for him. When I visited in 2012, eight of the visitors' notebooks were full of messages and illustrations, mostly about *Hakuōki*. This indicates that *Hakuōki* prompted female fans

Figure 1 The message reads: 'I love Tōdō Heisuke! This is my first visit to Mibu Temple! I'm sure I'll come back!' (25 Oct. 2011, photo: author)

to visit these sites in search of connections to historical figures via their favourite fictional characters.

Just as in reality, the Shinsengumi members in *Hakuōki* fight to the death as rebels against forces loyal to the Emperor. Part of the attraction of the characters is that they are historical losers. The sympathy of many *rekijo* with losers is also evident in *Sengoku BASARA*, particularly regarding Ishida Mitsunari and

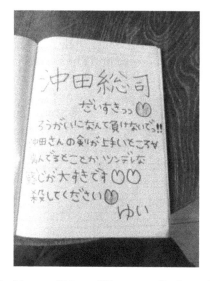

Figure 2 Yui addresses Okita as if he were still alive (photo: author)

Figure 3 The message reads: 'I love Sōji' (27 Aug. 2011, photo: author).

Chōsokabe Motochika. Ishida, the closest subordinate of Toyotomi Hideyoshi, was executed as a rebel leader by Tokugawa Ieyasu after defeat in the Battle of Sekigahara in 1600. Ishida's hometown (Ishida town in Nagahama, Shiga) attracted little attention from tourists until 1941, when the tombstones of the Ishidas were discovered underground at Hachiman Shrine (later renamed as Ishida Shrine). A memorial was built for Ishida Mitsunari, but it received only two or three visitors a month and they were usually middle-aged men (*Asahi shinbun* 2009a). However, tourism in Ishida town changed markedly with the growing numbers of young female visitors attracted there by two NHK Taiga dramas – *Tenchijin* (2009) and *Go* (2011) – and *Sengoku BASARA*. In November 2009, for example, over 160 people attended the memorial ceremony for Mitsunari, which few had attended before. Eighty per cent of the attendees were women (*Asahi shinbun* 2009b). Visitor numbers per year to Ishida town in search of Mitsunari sites increased to over 1,000 around 2009, and approximately 90 per cent of them were women (*Asahi shinbun* 2009a).

In *Sengoku BASARA,* Mitsunari is characterised as a young, handsome and faithful, but also furious man taking revenge on Masamune and Ieyasu. A 23-year-old female fan of Mitsunari wrote: 'Mitsunari is cute because he goes after Toyotomi Hideyoshi [like a dog] in the videogame' (*Yomiuri shinbun* 2011b). Mitsunari's portrayal in the videogame and the anime eliminates the negative images of him produced by 'traditional history'.

Re-evaluation of the losers is also evident regarding Chōsokabe Motochika. Motochika was the *daimyō* (feudal lord) who controlled Shikoku until he was defeated by Hideyoshi. He was almost unknown before the release of *Sengoku BASARA,* which represents Motochika as a young, handsome, and thoughtful 'older brother' (*aniki*). Due to the popularity of Motochika caused by *Sengoku BASARA,* Wakamiya Hachimangu Shrine in Kochi, where his statue stands, has seen a drastic rise in visitors:

> On the visitors' notebook placed near the statue, fans from all over Japan leave their messages. The increase in young female visitors is striking. The messages say: 'You are shining, *aniki*'. 'One of the coolest in Japan'. They address him as if he were an *aidoru* ['idol', namely a popular model, actor or singer].... Motochika's sudden popularity is due to *Sengoku BASARA,* which portrays Sengoku period samurai as *ikemen* [hunks].

> (*Yomiuri shinbun* 2010)

Such heritage tourism by *rekijo*, induced by *Sengoku BASARA,* has affected local communities. The Chōsokabe Motochika Fan Club was established in Motoyama town in January 2009. Kochi Prefectural Museum of History in Nangoku city set up regular exhibits about Chōsokabe that April. The curator said: 'This exhibition was produced with nationwide support from fans of Motochika. We want to display documents about his life so that we can satisfy young people's curiosity' (*Yomiuri shinbun* 2010). In 2011, approximately 150 visitors came to the twelfth Motochika Uijinsai (First Campaign Festival), the majority of whom were young women (*Yomiuri shinbun* 2011a). In 2012, the first Chōsokabe Festival was held by the Kochi Prefectural Government (The Tourist Office 2012).

Discussing the craze among *rekijo* for losers, Sakai (2008, p. 227) suggests that 'in the Sengoku period, samurai were filled with ambition. *Rekijo* sympathize with those who had tragic ends before fulfilling their ambitions. That creates intimacy and stimulates *rekijos*' maternal instincts, a feeling of "I want to support him."' In a manner similar to the mirage tour, it can be seen that *rekijo* in the 2000s long for psychological connections (*kankeisei*) with dead historical figures after seeing portrayals of those figures as young and handsome characters in videogames and anime.

Nurturing pop-spiritualism among women through heritage tourism

As mentioned above, the heritage tourism of *rekijo* induced by pop-cultural forms is often motivated by their search for psychological connections to characters and historical figures. One might assume that such factors can be also observed in male-centred anime pilgrimage. In the case of *Lucky star*, as Satō (2009, p. 77) suggests, Washimiya Shrine has become the centre of pilgrimage for fans because the shrine is not only the location used in the anime but also fictionally related to its characters. However, the characters in *Lucky star* are completely fictional, so the type of spiritualism exhibited by *rekijo* does not exist between the fans and the characters. The location used in *Lucky star* happens to be a real shrine. But, it could equally have been a school, store or just an open field. *Rekijo* pilgrimage, by contrast, is closely connected to spiritualism in that *rekijo* seek connections with dead historical figures, some of whom are enshrined as deities at the shrines and temples *rekijo* visit. Historical facts and historical sites (tombs, temples, shrines, castles and so on) stimulate the imaginations of *rekijo*, through which they can perceive and construct psychological connections to their favourite historical figures. A desire to construct a spiritual connection is more conspicuous in *rekijo* tourism than in men's contents tourism.

Spiritualism is defined as '(1) the view that spirit is a prime element of reality, and (2) a belief that spirits of the dead communicate with the living usually through a medium' (Spiritualism 2011). Although associated with occult ideas, shamanism or animism, this sort of spiritualism is also inherent within Shinto and Japanese Buddhism. In recent years, young people with no deep faith in Shinto or Buddhism seem to readily accept the existence of *kami* (gods), deity power, ghosts and spirits of the dead. Kayama (2006, pp. 111–116), a psychiatrist and critic, suggests that many of her female clients are unsatisfied with her diagnosis that their sufferings have resulted from societal and political problems, and they crave something spiritual that reassures them, something that 'accepts one the way one is'. She states that feminist counselling used to address the personal problems of women by reducing them to societal and political problems, but this type of counselling is no longer convincing to many female clients. Against the backdrop of recession and widening social inequality, those with personal issues long not for logical explanations or solutions, but for unconditional acceptance by spiritual beings.

This superficial spiritualism is similar to the growing nationalistic or patriotic actions and sentiments of young people. Referring to the pop-nationalism of young people, as seen in their support for the Japanese national football team or consumption of pop culture such as manga, Sakamoto suggests that '"[p]op" nationalism is about ordinary people's modes of relating to the nation-state and it is often mediated by the dynamics of mass/popular culture. It relies heavily on images and icons that are cut-off from their historical meanings' (2008 [2007], p. 10). Kayama called this tendency among young people 'petit nationalism syndrome' (2002, pp. 27–28). Kayama argues that fervent, young fans of the Japanese national team at the 2002 FIFA World Cup, for instance, did not connect their nationalistic or patriotic actions and sentiments to any historical context or ideology. They never imagined that their behaviour was connected to wartime patriotism or right-wing attitudes.

Sakamoto also argues that the ahistorical and apolitical nature of pop-nationalism derives from 'the loss of meaning and identity in advanced capitalist/consumer societies and also the high level of uncertainty that has characterized Japan's post-bubble economy' (2008 [2007], p. 2). In a similar manner, my definition of 'popular spiritualism' is the acceptance of and enthusiasm for spiritual power, deity or something supernatural in those who have little religious faith, while the physical desires for money, status and possessing commodities are still pursued.

A 'pop-spiritualist' atmosphere has been substantially nurtured through TV shows, such as those featuring Gibo Aiko and Ehara Hiroyuki, and through Kagawa Nami's books and seminars from the late 1980s until the early 2000s. In the late 1980s and the early 1990s, the bubble economy and its aftermath imprinted social uncertainty and instability on the minds of young people. In the early 1990s, a housewife psychic, Gibo Aiko, often appeared in TV shows, reading guests' previous lives by observing their ancestors' dead spirits and the evil spirits that negatively affect them. Growing interest in spiritualism generated by TV was demonstrated in the sales of her books and the increase in the number of programmes featuring Gibo, such as the TBS series *Gibo Aiko the amazing psychic* (*Kyōi no reinōsha Gibo Aiko*) in the early 1990s. However, in the same shows, scientists such as Professor Ōtsuki Yoshihiko of Waseda University often appeared as guests and cast doubt on the truth of her statements. The juxtaposition of spiritualism and science prevented the shows having an occultist atmosphere and turned them into entertainment. The Gibo boom ended around 1995, when the Aum religious cult's sarin gas attack on the Tokyo subway exposed the dangers of spiritualism.

In the 2000s, however, spiritualism was revived by Ehara Hiroyuki, albeit in a casual manner. A psychic and Shinto priest, Ehara calls himself a *supirichuaru kaunserā* (spiritual counsellor) to avoid using the Japanese term for spiritualism, *shinreishugi*, which has negative connotations (Kayama 2006, p. 72, Tomabechi 2007, pp. 55–56). His successful TV programme *The spring of Aura* (*Ōra no izumi*, 2005–2010) on the Asahi TV network was co-hosted by Miwa Akihiro, a well-known cross-dressing singer/actor, and Kokubun Taichi, a member of boy band TOKIO. It started as a late-night show in 2005, but its popularity meant it was moved to prime time in 2007. In a manner similar to Gibo, Ehara reads the spirits of guests' ancestors and sometimes subdues evil spirits. However, unlike the programmes in which Gibo appeared, no scientific voices were included in *The spring of Aura*. Ehara also limited himself to counselling, and did not insist on the truth of his spiritual statements. His stance alleviated scepticism and fears regarding spiritualism among young people, especially young women who crave to be accepted the way they are (Kayama 2006, p. 115). Indeed, Ehara's seminars are always full of young female participants.

Kagawa Nami, meanwhile, whose nickname is Miracle-happy Nami-chan, has published books aimed at young people about how to become comfortable psychologically as well as financially, such as *A spiritual way to make money* (*Omoshiroi hodo okane wo hikiyoseru kokoro no mochikata*, 2011). According to Kayama (2006, p. 73), Kagawa's affirmation of materialism allowed young women to accept her spiritualism easily. Popularized spiritualism, or 'pop-spiritualism', therefore, is a means for young women to accept themselves through the affirmation of their ancestors' spirits or by putting the blame for present misfortunes on their deeds in their previous lives, without changing their materialistic lifestyle.

This 'healing' effect of pop-spiritualism that bridges the past and the present is evident in *rekijo* pilgrimage in the 2000s. The pilgrimages by fans of *Mirage of blaze*, *Sengoku BASARA* and *Hakuōki* to historical sites related to their favourite characters connect the fictional characters in the anime to the fans' reality. Such pilgrimages have gained popularity among fans. For example, in June 2009 JTB sold a tour targeting young women, '*Sengoku BASARA*: Date's Troop Tour', in which tourists visited places related to Date Masamune and Katakura Kojūrō (Date's closest subordinate). It sold out immediately and about 90 per cent of participants were women (Oricon life 2009).

As mentioned above, pilgrimage by women to historical sites induced by mass media products was observed well before the 2000s. Nor is it exclusive to the Japanese either. However, the pilgrimage triggered by *Mirage of blaze*, *Sengoku BASARA* and *Hakuōki* differs from conventional contents tourism in that the female travellers repeatedly visit historical sites – not only castles and tombs, but also religious sites such as Shinto shrines and Buddhist temples – to construct *kankeisei* (connectedness). Most feudal lords of the Sengoku Period were enshrined in Shinto shrines. *Rekijo*, therefore, will visit Uesugi Shrine, where Uesugi Kenshin was enshrined, or fans of Date Masamune and *Sengoku BASARA* will leave messages on *ema* (wooden votive plaques) to both fictional characters and real historical figures at Miyagi Gokoku Shrine (Iwai 2009, p. 47). Their actions suggest that they are attempting to connect fictional characters to historical reality, constructing the belief that they can feel the existence of the dead spirits of their favourite samurai.

Furthermore, through these practices, an idealized and imagined 'Japanese identity' and 'Japanese-ness' is constructed without truly integrating historical or ideological backgrounds. Suzuki argues that 'in order to analyse our concept of Japan, decentralization, and localization and re-examine our values and aesthetics, it is vital to consider Japanese "history"' (2009, p. 21). The search for 'Japan' in Japanese history nurtures respect for and leads people to re-value their ancestors, which leads to the affirmation of the 'self' as Japanese.

Conclusion

This article has explored the *rekijo* phenomenon by examining the relationship between young women and heritage tourism in the 1970s, TV-induced historical tourism of women in the 1980s, the mirage tour prompted by *Mirage of blaze* in the 1990s and contemporary women's pilgrimage induced by *Sengoku BASARA* and *Hakuōki* in the 2000s–2010s.

In the 1970s, women's heritage tourism was primarily induced by mass media such as fashion magazines and TV advertisements which promoted the construction of 'Japanese-ness'. It also served to challenge Japanese gender norms.

Although the media-led trends in women's historical tourism continued in the 1980s, the search for connections with historical figures via their representations in TV dramas and films became an important driving force. The tragic ends of historical losers enabled women to sympathize with historical figures, which eventually nurtured their respect for dead spirits.

During the 1990s, popular culture underwent a massive transition with the development of the internet and a 'mixed-media strategy'. The Mirage Tour undertaken by *mirajennu* was generated by a narrative in which spiritualism, *goryō shinkō* (the folk religious belief in vengeful sprits), adolescent hardships, healing and boys' love were blended to produce diverse ways for female fans to derive pleasure and entertainment. The mirage tour served as a way for young women to construct *kankeisei* with characters, historical figures and themselves. The search for their psychological connections extended to the construction of online networks among *mirajennu*.

In the 2000s, female history fans were 'discovered'. They were named *rekijo* in a postfeminist context and were expected to become potential customers helping Japan out of its long-lasting recession. Their gender-crossover activities appeared to be symbols of gender equality (Sugiura 2005). However, the driving force behind *rekijo* pilgrimage is the relationships (*kankeisei*) between fictional characters, historical figures and themselves. The pleasure of *rekijo* in constructing connections between the three emerged in the context of 'pop-spiritualism' in the 2000s. This 'pop-spiritualism' is a hybrid phenomenon combining Shinto, Buddhism and *goryō shinkō* with TV-mediated non-religious spiritualism. This was demonstrated by the 'pilgrimage' of female fans of *Sengoku BASARA* and *Hakuōki*. *Rekijo* are not particularly religious or conscious of the connection of Shinto with wartime nationalism, rather they worship the dead spirits of their favourite historical losers via the representations of them in popular cultural forms such as *Sengoku BASARA* and *Hakuōki*. Their '"pop" nationalistic' faith towards Shinto's *kami* and Buddha, what I call 'pop-spiritualism', contributes to a re-evaluation of their 'Japanese-ness'. These re-conceptualized conservative views in part explain women's nostalgia for Japanese traditional gender images, but also simultaneously why they take pleasure in relating their own realities to an idealized past, constructing *kankeisei* with fictional characters, actual historical figures, themselves and, what is more, other *rekijo* through SNSs, blogs and *dōjinshi*.

In pop-nationalism, Sakamoto suggests,

consuming the 'nation' as a depoliticized icon alleviates the pain of oppression in a highly 'managed' society, compensates for the uncertain sense of self, and creates an imaginary connection with the other atomized individuals in the urban, often dehumanized, life-worlds of today's generations.

(Sakamoto 2008 [2007], p. 2)

Similarly, in the pop-spiritualism evident in the texts and comments of *rekijo* analysed in this article, the supernatural and its representations in pop-cultural narratives based on historical fact serve as a site in which they consume and take pleasure in establishing *kankeisei* by connecting the virtual world and their reality. They are not profoundly interested in religion and nationalism. Nevertheless, *kankeisei* and pop-spiritualism are significant factors in understanding the ways in which *rekijo* enjoy heritage tourism.

Notes

1. A volunteer guide at Ise Jingu Shrine told me in January 2011 that many young women had mistaken trees in front of the gate of the main sanctuary for the 'power spot' and pressed themselves against them, seriously damaging the bark. Since then, the trees have been protected by long bamboo boards, which prevent any visitors from touching the bark.
2. *Mirajennu* combines the word 'mirage' with the French suffix −enne, as in Parisienne. Members of the all-female Takarazuka theatre troop are called *takarajennu* and this inspired the term *mirajennu*.
3. The proportion of women in the intake of universities and two-year colleges in 1965 was 11.3 per cent, but in 1975 it went up to 32.9 per cent (Higher Education Bureau 2009, p. 13).
4. Sōji (a shorten form of Sōjirō) is often pronounced as Sōshi in TV dramas and films. It sounds more sophisticated in Japanese.
5. The series aimed to compete with the *Red and white song contest*, the New Year's Eve institution on NHK. The first drama, *Chūshingura* recorded the highest viewing figures (15.3 per cent) on the commercial channels in this time slot (*Yomiuri shinbun* 1986), although the viewing figures did not surpass those of NHK's *Song contest*.
6. Light novels (*raito noberu*) are a genre of juvenile literature. They often contain manga-style illustrations of characters and settings. However, in the 1990s, when the *Mirage of blaze* series was serialized in *Cobalt* girls' monthly magazine, the term 'light novel' had not yet been coined.
7. 'Boys' love' (BL) is an umbrella term for works that depict male-male homosexual fantasy in the forms of manga, novels, anime and videogames. They are produced primarily by women and aimed at women. This term has been used since around 1993 when *Magazine Be x Boy*, a manga magazine about BL, was published (Sugiura 2006).

References

Akagi, Y., 2007. *'An-an' 1970*. Tokyo: Heibonsha.

Anon., 2010. 47 todōfuken no pawā supotto. *CREA*, March, 26−116.

Arase, T., 2011. Utsunomiya himitsu meguri tsuā. Available from: http://www.city.utsunomiya. tochigi.jp/dbps_data/_material_/localhost/sougouseisaku/shiseikenkyucenter/ H22himitumeguri.pdf [Accessed 23 Aug. 2012].

The Art Newspaper, 2010. Exhibition and museum attendance figures 2009. April, 23−30. Available from: http://www.theartnewspaper.com/attfig/attfig09.pdf [Accessed 12 June 2014].

Asahi shinbun, 1997. Enshoku no wain, Geikousei ga shōhin kikaku: Uesugi matsuri mae ni gentei hanbai. *Asahi shinbun* (Yamagata edn), 20 April, n.p.

Asahi shinbun, 2008. Chishō Naoe Kanetsugu sokuseki wo tazunete: 15− Samegaojō atoni 'saigo no shokuji' Niigataken. *Asahi shinbun*, 12 June, p. 34.

Asahi shinbun, 2009a. Oshiyoseru rekijo: gēmu de jinbutsuzō ni kyōkan. *Asahi shinbun*, 20 May, p. 25.

Asahi shinbun, 2009b. Koisuru hito wa sengoku bushō: 'rekijo' senjin, kotō/kohoku no machi genkini, Shiga. *Asahi shinbun*, 9 Dec., p. 34.

Asahi shinbun, 2010a. Hijikata Toshizō ni chakumoku 'rekijo' yobikome Utsunomiya himitsu meguri tsuā. *Asahi shinbun* (Tochigi edn), 24 Sept., p. 35.

Asahi shinbun, 2010b. 860 mannin ga Ise mairi: kako saikō, 'pawā supotto' kōka? *Asahi shinbun*, 20 Dec. Available from: http://www.asahi.com/travel/news/NGY201012200009.html [Accessed 6 March 2011].

Byakko tai, 1986. TV, NTV, 30–31 Dec.

Cabinet Office, 2009. *White Paper on Gender Equality 2009*. Available from: http://www8.cao.go.jp/survey/h21/h21-danjo/index.html [Accessed 12 June 2014].

Fuji Film, 2010. Rekishi būmu nimiru shinbijinesu no kitai. *Club GC*, 10 June. Available from: https://www.net-fbs.com/dyn/member/gc/gr/1006/index.html [Accessed 12 June 2014].

Fukazawa, M., 2009. Fukazawa Maki no heisei joshi zukan: rekijo to wajoshi. *Nikkei Business Online*, 20 Sept. Available from: http://business.nikkeibp.co.jp/article/skillup/20090520/195263 [Accessed 12 June 2014].

Gintama, 2006–2010, 2011–2012. TV, TV Tokyo, April 2006–March 2010, April 2011–March 2012.

Gotō, B., 1973. *Nosutoradamusu no daiyogen*. Tokyo: Shōbunsha.

Hakuōki, 2010. TV, Tokyo MX, April–June.

Hakuōki Hekketsuroku, 2010. TV, Tokyo MX. Oct.–Dec.

Hakuōki Reimeiroku, 2012. TV, Tokyo MX. July–Sept.

Hamana, K., 2009. Arasā, arafō 'butsuzō joshi' uttori: honne wa iyashi? Yomiuri shinbun, 26 Sept., p. 13.

Hashimoto, H., 2006. Matsuri: Tsukurareru tabi. *In*: Oda Kōji, ed. *Kankō no shakai shinrigaku*. Kyoto: Kitaōjishobō, 167–183.

Hayashi, M., 2005. Disukabā japan kyanpēn niokeru kankō no shiten to taishō nikansuru kenkyū. Available from: http://www.soc.titech.ac.jp/publication/Theses2005/master/03M43228.pdf [Accessed 12 June 2014].

Henshūbu, ed., 1998. *Honō no mirāju wo meguru: mirāju foto kikō higashi nihon hen*. Tokyo: Shūeisha.

Higher Education Bureau, Ministry of Education, Culture, Sports, Science and Technology, Japan, 2009. Daigaku no ryōteki kibonado ni kansuru shiryō. 14 April. Available from: http://www.mext.go.jp/b_menu/shingi/chukyo/chukyo4/siryo/__icsFiles/afieldfile/2009/05/08/1262948_4.pdf [Accessed 12 June 2014].

Inoue, N., 1999. *Wakamono to gendai shūkyō: ushinawareta zahyōjiku*. Tokyo: Chikuma shobō.

Iwai, T., 2009. Rekishi-kei gēmu, rekishi-kei anime no hensen to 'rekijo' wo umidasu mekanizumu. *Chōsajōhō*, Sept.–Oct. 490, 46–49.

JTB, 2010. Sengoku bushō yukarinochi wo tazunete. Available from: http://www.jtb.co.jp/kokunai/pkg/basara [Accessed 12 June 2014].

Kagawa, N., 2011. *Omoshiroihodo okane wo hikiyoseru kokoro no mochikata*. Tokyo: PHP Shuppan.

Kawaguchi, Y., 2010. BL, rekijo – otaku joshi no shinsekai: watashitachi minna 'otome' moe! *Aera*, 26 July, 44–47.

Kayama, R., 2002. *Puchi nashonarizumu shōkōgun: wakamonotachi no nippon shugi*. Tokyo: Chūōkōronsha.

Kayama, R., 2006. *Supirichuaru ni hamaru hito, hamaranai hito*. Tokyo: Gentōsha.

Kensei e-shinbun, 2010. 'Oumiji rekijo burogā tabi kikō' sankasha kettei! 31 Aug. Available from: http://www.pref.shiga.jp/hodo/e-shinbun/fb01/20100831.html [Accessed 30 Nov. 2010].

Kihei tai, 1989. TV, NTV. 30–31 Dec.

Kuwabara, M., 1992. *Honou no mirāju*, Vol. 8, *Hasha no makyō III*. Tokyo: Shūeisha.

Kuwabara, M., 1993. *Honou no mirāju*, Vol. 11, *Wadatsumi no Yōkihi chūhen*. Tokyo: Shūeisha.

Kuwabara, M., 1994. *Honou no mirāju*, Vol. 14, *Yomi eno fūketsu kōhen*. Tokyo: Shūeisha.

Kuwabara, M., 2001. *Honou no mirāju wo meguru: mirāju foto kikō nishi nihon hen*. Tokyo: Shūeisha.

Kuwabara, M., 2005 [1992]. *Honou no mirāju*, Vol. 2, *Aka no zan'ei*. Tokyo: Shūeisha.

Masubuchi, T., 2010. *Monogatari wo tabisuru hitobito: kontentsu tsūrizumu towa nanika*. Tokyo: Sairyūsha.

Ministry of Health, Labour, and Welfare, 2010. Heisei 21nendo ban: Hataraku josei no jitsujō. Available from: http://www.mhlw.go.jp/bunya/koyoukintou/josei-jitsujo/dl/09d.pdf [Accessed 12 June 2014].

Mirage tour community, 2012. SNS mixi. Available from: http://mixi.jp/view_community.pl?id=1041393 [Accessed 13 Sept. 2012].

Moeyo ken, 1970. TV, NET (TV Asahi). April–Sept.

Nakamura, A., 2009. Imadoki gēmu jijō Nakamura Akinori: 'rekijo' tte nanda? Sengoku akushon gēmu wo torimaku doukou wo tetteikaimei! *Gamebusiness.jp*, 17 June. Available from: http://www.gamebusiness.jp/article.php?id=36 [Accessed 12 June 2014].

Nakano, Hiroya, 2009. 'Rekijo' no koigokoro wo kusugureba. *21 seiki Wakayama*, (58). Available from: http://magoichi.or.tv/machiokoshi/58kikou.htm [Accessed 12 June 2014].

Okita Sōshi, 1974. Film. Directed by Masanobu Deme. Japan: Tōhō.

Oricon life, 2009. 'Sengoku BASARA' no kyara kiyō: 'rekijo' nimuketa bushō junrei gaidobon hatsubai. 3 Sept. Available from: http://life.oricon.co.jp/68856/full/ [Accessed 12 June 2014].

Saitō, M., 2001 [2000]. *Modan gāru ron: onnanoko niwa shusse no michi ga futatsu aru*. Tokyo: Magazine House.

Saitō, T., 2009. *Kankeisuru onna shoyūsuru otoko*. Tokyo: Kōdansha.

Sakai, H., 2008. Fushigi hitto wo kiru 45: sengokubushō. *Nikkei Trendy*, (4), 226–227.

Sakamoto, K., 1999. Reading Japanese women's magazines: the construction of new identities in the 1970s and 1980s. *Media, Culture and Society*, 21 (2), 173–193.

Sakamoto, R., 2008 [2007]. Will you go to war? Or will you stop being Japanese? Nationalism and history in Kobayashi Yoshinori's Sensōron. *In*: Michael Heazle and Nick Knight, eds. *China-Japan relations in the twenty-first century: creating a future past?* Cheltenham: Edward Elgar. Posted at Japan Focus. 14 Jan. Available from: http://japanfocus.org/-Rumi-SAKAMOTO/2632 [Accessed 12 June 2014].

Satō, Y., 2009. Ikanishite jinja wa seichi to nattaka: kōkyōsei to hinichijō ga umidasu seichi no hatten. *In*: Cultural Resource Management Research Team, ed. *CATS Library 1: Media to kontentsu tsūrizumu*. Center for Advanced Tourism Studies, Hokkaido University, 71–84.

Sengoku BASARA, 2009. TV, TBS. April–June.

Sengoku BASARA II, 2010. TV, TBS. July–Sept.

Sengoku BASARA the last party, 2011. Film. Dir. Kazuya Nomura. Japan: Shōchiku.

Shinada, H., 2009. Josei ga ashura ni uttori. Butsuzō ten wo miniitta! *Nikkei Trendy* [online]. 20 April, 1–7. Available from: http://trendy.nikkeibp.co.jp/article/column/20090415/1025472/?ST=life&P=1 [Accessed 14 June 2014].

Shinsengumi!, 2004. TV, NHK. Jan.–Dec.

Shinsengumi keppū roku, 1965–1966. TV, NET (TV Asahi). July 1965–Jan. 1966.

Shinsengumi keppū roku, 1998. TV, TV Asahi., Oct.–Dec.

Shirakawa, T., 2009. Naze 20 dai kōgakureki joshi wa 'sengyōshufu' nerai nanoka. *President*, 29 June, 68–75.

Spiritualism, 2011. *Merriam-Webster Dictionary*. Available from: http://www.merriam-webster.com/dictionary/spiritualism?show=0&t=1300523904 [Accessed 14 June 2014].

Sugiura, Y., 2005. Moeru onna otaku otoko no gajō ni shinshutsu. *AERA*, 20 June, 46–50.

Sugiura, Y., 2006. *Otaku joshi kenkyū: fujoshi shisō taikei*. Tokyo: Harashobō.

Suzuki, K., 2009. Disukabā japan no sairaika: rekishi būmu wa 'josei' ga tsukuru. *Chōsajōhō*, Sept.–Oct. (490), 20–21.

Tenchijin, 2009. TV, NHK. Jan.–Nov.

Tōge no Gunzō, 1982. TV, NHK. Jan.–Dec.

Tomabechi, H., 2007. *Spiritualism*. Tokyo: Ningen Shuppan.

The Tourist Office, Kochi city government, 2012. Dai 1 kai Chōsokabe matsuri. 12 April. Available from: http://www.city.kochi.kochi.jp/soshiki/39/chosokabematsuri-1.html [Accessed 14 June 2014].

Yomiuri shinbun, 1982a. Edo kara Showa e: Tokyo no shiseki wo aruku – Sengakuji. *Yomiuri shinbun*, 13 Dec., p. 21.

Yomiuri shinbun, 1982b. Fukyō e uchiiri da: Gishisai, Kirasai ni 5mannin. *Yomiuri shinbun*, 15 Dec., p. 20.

Yomiuri shinbun, 1986. *Byakko tai* NHK kōhaku ni kirikomu. *Yomiuri shinbun*, 13 Dec., p. 6.

Yomiuri shinbun, 2010. Natsukusa no fu: Motochika no gōki wakamono miryō, Kōchi. *Yomiuri shinbun*, 2 Dec., p. 28.

Yomiuri shinbun, 2011a. Rekijora kōfun! Motochika 'uijinsai' Kōchi, Wakamiyajinja. *Yomiuri shinbun*, 23 May, p. 28.

Yomiuri shinbun, 2011b. Ikemen bushō no katana shōkai: Nagafune hakubutsukan ni 50ten, 'rekijo' ni ninki. *Yomiuri shinbun*, 24 July, p. 25.

Akiko Sugawa-Shimada is an associate professor in the Department of Human Science, Yokohama National University. She is the author of a number of articles on anime and popular culture, including 'Grotesque cuteness of *Shōjo*: representations of *Goth-Loli* in Japanese contemporary TV *Anime*' in *Japanese Animation: East Asian Perspectives* (University Press of Mississippi, 2013), *Girls and magic: representations of magical girls and Japanese female viewership* (NTT Shuppan, 2013), 'Fruits basket' in *The survey of graphic novels: manga* (Salem Press, 2012) and 'Rebel with causes and laughter for relief: 'essay manga' of Tenten Hosokawa and Rieko Saibara, and Japanese female readership' in *Journal of Graphic Novels and Comics* (2011).

Contents tourism and local community response: *Lucky star* and collaborative anime-induced tourism in Washimiya

TAKAYOSHI YAMAMURA

Abstract: This article demonstrates how a local community succeeded in forming favourable relationships with fans and copyright holders in Washimiya, a town in which the anime television series *Lucky star* was set. Washimiya is now visited by fans from all across Japan as a so-called anime sacred site. Through interviews with fans, local people and the anime production company, participant observation and analysis of primary documents, the article outlines how the local community, fans and copyright holders formed relationships based on mutual consideration to the benefit of all. Mutual understanding and common goals emerged from their shared respect for the contents (*Lucky star*), a phenomenon that has received little attention in discussions about 'contents tourism'. By viewing contents tourism not only as a licensing business or business between the host and the guest, but instead as communication between people in an actual space and time with contents at the centre of interactions, many important insights are gained into the potential for contents tourism.

Introduction

The phenomena of film-induced tourism, literature-induced tourism and other forms of media-induced tourism have long been recognized within the field of tourism studies. In Japan, the term *kontentsu tsūrizumu* (contents tourism) brings together all these different forms of media-induced tourism. This article explores how a local community can launch a regional development programme (defined in this article as 'a programme aiming to revitalize a local community economically, socially and culturally') through contents tourism, specifically anime-induced tourism. There is no model answer to this question as each case differs according to production processes, the conditions under which the anime was broadcast and local policy. However, previous studies, such as Horiuchi (2010), have identified that the key for local communities is how well they can formulate favourable relationships with fans and the copyright holders.

This article examines how a local community succeeded in forming favourable relationships among these actors in the Washimiya district of Kuki city, Saitama prefecture.[1] This town was the location for the anime television series *Lucky star*. It is visited by fans from all over Japan and is one of the so-called 'anime sacred sites', *anime seichi*, defined by Yamamura as 'a location in an animated work or a place related to the work or author whose value is acknowledged by fans' (2008, p. 146).

Lucky star is a four-frame manga series by Yoshimizu Kagami which also became a computer game and anime television series. The original four-frame manga was serialized in *Comptiq*, a monthly game and manga magazine published by Kadokawa Shoten Publishing Co. Ltd (hereafter 'Kadokawa'), starting in January 2004. The animated TV series was produced by Kyoto Animation and broadcast in twenty-four episodes from April to September 2007 by sixteen TV stations, most of which were independent UHF stations.

The manga depicts the mundane daily life of four high school girls and the people around them. Two of the girls, Hiiragi Kagami and Hiiragi Tsukasa, are the daughters of the Shinto priest of Takamiya Shrine. In the animated TV version, Takamiya Shrine is modelled on Washinomiya Shrine in Washimiya town.

The number of fans visiting Washimiya town as a result of seeing the anime was unprecedented. With the collaboration of local communities, fans and copyright holders, the visits of fans developed into a town revitalization programme. There are two main reasons why the anime induced such levels of tourism.

First, the opening scene of each episode, which recreated actual scenes in the town, made an extremely strong impression on viewers. Every episode, viewers watched the same opening scene, which was an effective combination of high-quality graphic background images, the story's characters and a catchy theme song. This opening left a powerful impression of the scenery of Washimiya town on viewers (Yamamura 2012).

Second, this show was a representative example of a genre of animation in which descriptions of deep personal relationships or fully fledged romantic relationships are deliberately eliminated from the story in order to tell a light, non-serious story that focuses on the everyday lives and conversations of the *bishōjo* (young, pretty girl) characters. Consequently, the fans, local community and copyright holders were able to create connections with an actual location and the *bishōjo* characters in various ways without being tied up by the story, and they were able to vitalize communication through the characters (Uno 2011, pp. 382–392; Yamamura 2011a). In other words, the lack of dramatic aspects in the plot enabled a type of tourism in which reality is sought by linking the anime to actual locations. This genre of anime is called 'daily life anime' (*nichijo-kei*) or 'slice of life anime' (*kūki-kei*, literally 'air style'). Anime shows of this genre have been produced in large numbers since the mid-2000s.

Contents tourism and tourism policy

Contents tourism is attracting increasing attention in the context of tourism policy formation. In the past few years, the Japanized English expression 'contents tourism' has spread throughout Japan. The first public use of this term was in 2005 when three governmental organizations, the Ministry of Land, Infrastructure, Transport and Tourism (MLIT), the Ministry of Economy, Trade and Industry (METI) and the Agency for Cultural Affairs, released the jointly prepared 'Investigative Report on Regional Development by the Production and Utilization of Contents such as Film' (Ministry of Land, Infrastructure, Transport and Tourism *et al.* 2005).

In this report, from a policy perspective, contents tourism is defined as 'tourism with the intention of promoting travel and related industries by utilizing contents related to the local area (movies, television dramas, novels, manga, games and so on)' (p. 49). It also says that the essence of the approach is 'the addition of a "narrative quality" [*monogatarisei*] or "theme" [*tēmasei*] to a region – namely an atmosphere or image particular to the region generated by the contents – and the use of that narrative quality as a tourism resource'. This report was revolutionary in that it sent a message to local governments that at the heart of tourism promotion was not 'objects' but 'contents', namely stories.

The introduction to the report gives three main reasons for its publication. First, local governments and economic associations were becoming increasingly aware of increases in tourists numbers when a movie, drama or anime was set in a certain locality. This phenomenon became particularly clear in connection with the Korean TV drama, *Winter sonata*, broadcast on NHK BS2 from April to September 2003. The drama was hugely popular among middle-aged and older Japanese women and a large number of Japanese tourists visited the drama locations in South Korea. This phenomenon and the economic ripple effects are introduced in the report (p. 52), which demonstrates the large amount of attention it attracted inside the government.

Second, the 'Action plan for becoming a tourism destination country' (*Kankō rikkoku kōdō keikaku*) was formed by the government's Tourism Destination-related Ministerial Meeting in July 2003. Following this, support for the production and screening of Japanese movies (from the Ministry of Education, Culture, Sports, Science and Technology (MEXT)), support for the activities of film commissions and attracting film projects (from MEXT and MLIT) and the promotion of contents industries (from METI) were deemed to be important measures for promoting the attractiveness of localities and Japan as a whole, and for the overseas promotion of the Japanese brand.

Third, the government's Intellectual Property Strategy Headquarters drafted the '2004 intellectual property promotion plan' (Chiteki zaisan senryaku honbu 2004), which clearly stated that 'enhancing the preservation and dissemination of the attractive contents of localities and so on' should be part of a 'dramatic enlargement of the contents business' (pp. 78, 94).

This report views contents tourism from the perspective of the localities and stresses that localities should strategically 'utilize' movies, dramas, anime and other forms of contents as tourism resources.

Anime pilgrimage and regional promotion

The emergence of verifiable cases of pilgrimage to anime sacred sites by fans has led to a growth in regional promotion based on anime and other contents. While the MLIT report (2005) described the significance of localities strategically utilizing anime and other contents as tourism resources, a successful case of contents tourism emerged in 2007 in a way completely unexpected to officials and with no relation to the tourism-promotion strategies of central and local government.

Following the airing of the anime television series *Lucky star* in 2007 fans spontaneously began to visit Washimiya. Gradually a partnership was formed between the locality and the contents copyright holders, and this developed into a regional promotion policy.

Washimiya is situated in northeast Saitama and had a population of approximately 34,000 in 2006.[2] It used to have hardly any tourism but the town suddenly began receiving domestic and foreign tourists after being used as a location for *Lucky star*. Led by the local Commerce and Industry Association, the community organized various activities with the cooperation of the copyright holders that succeeded in thrilling the fans. It developed into a form of regional promotion based on the cooperation of the local community and fans. The mass media gave wide coverage to this success story of a small, little-known town developing into a popular tourist site visited by many young people, all because of an anime.

With the help of such coverage, the profile of various sites, but particularly Washinomiya Shrine (which appeared in the opening scene of the anime) became dramatically higher. The number of people making *hatsumōde* New Year's shrine visits (in the first three days of the new year) was only 90,000 prior to the airing of the anime, but, according to a survey by the Saitama Prefectural Police, it increased by about 3.5-fold in three years to 300,000 in 2008, 420,000 in 2009 and 450,000 in 2010.

There had been other similar cases of anime and manga contents playing roles in the promotion of localities and shopping districts. Sakaiminato city in Tottori prefecture has been the most successful in attracting visitors over an extended period of time. Sakaiminato is the hometown of the well-known manga artist Mizuki Shigeru, and the city promotes its shopping district using his manga/anime Gegege-no-Kitaro. The locality, therefore, has had a nationally famous set of contents to use. The case of Washimiya, by contrast, was revolutionary in that fans and the locality worked together and built up the popularity of a little-known anime by a little-known writer.

No assessment of the power of contents to attract people to localities, particularly the 'tourism contents' spawning subcultures among anime and manga fans, had been carried out by tourism researchers or public administrations up to this point, despite the immense popularity of Japanese anime and manga abroad as well as in Japan. However, the Washimiya case demonstrated that subcultures created via anime and manga have high levels of appeal, especially to young adults both domestically and abroad, and have the power to attract people to the locality. By doing so they have the potential to stimulate the development of regional promotion policies. It is not an overstatement to say that *Lucky star* precipitated a paradigm shift in how people in both academic tourism research and central/local government view anime and manga.

This is evident in the reaction of the government. Following the success of *Lucky star*, METI and the Japan Tourism Agency began to organize meetings and forums to discuss the relationship between anime and tourism in which the Washimiya case was cited as a successful example.[3] Also, in response to the success of Washimiya, Saitama prefecture's Tourism Section in the Department of Industry and Labour established the Anime Tourism Review Committee in June 2009. It brought together experts from various fields and had the aim of promoting the prefecture's tourism using anime and manga (Saitama Prefecture 2009).

Methodological issues

Lucky star not only attracted a great number of visitors to Washimiya, it also had a great effect on the tourism policies of central and local governments. Therefore, the Washimiya case study provides significant scope for exploring the potential of contents tourism, especially relating to anime tourism and the relationship between attracting tourists and regional development.

Research into contents tourism is relatively new. Major works thus far include articles by Okamoto (2010, 2011) and books by Masubuchi (2010) and Yamamura (2011b). But no systematic academic discussions have been undertaken yet. Okamoto's research is innovative in that it proposes a framework for research into contents tourism based on his discussion of the actions of tourists using psychology and communication theory. However, it does not demonstrate the overall processes of regional promotion or the relationship between community and copyright holders. On the other hand, Masubuchi (2010) and Yamamura (2011b) introduce various case studies and/or propose a regional development model. These are useful because of their collection and presentation of detailed data. However, they are publications aimed at the general public and lack academic analysis. Other investigative reports by Yamamura (2008, 2011a) examine the circumstances leading to the regional development of Washimiya triggered by *Lucky star*, but these results are limited, too, in academic analysis.

This article discusses how contents tourism operates from the perspectives of the local community, the anime fans and the copyright holders. In addition, it demonstrates the importance of collaboration between the local community and fans and the local community and the copyright holders for contents tourism to contribute to regional development.

The main research methods in this article are interviews with fans, community members and those involved in the production of *Lucky star*, participant observation at events and literature review. Much of the information is from websites, newspapers and articles in general magazines because such topics relating to subculture are rarely discussed in academic sources. The article draws particularly on the websites of anime production companies, which tend to promote their anime by launching an official website and releasing the latest information via the website rather than through other media. Furthermore, fans create online communities and these websites are invaluable resources for grasping the trends and reactions of fans. The content of such sites, however, is constantly changing and the reliability of the information is not always guaranteed. Therefore, where possible this study refers to official sites.

The formation of the collaborative relationship between fans and the local community

The anime television series *Lucky star* was first broadcast in April 2007, and the *torii* (shrine gate) of Washinomiya Shrine and the tea house Otori-chaya appeared together with the main character Hiiragi Kagami in part of the opening sequence. The scene lasted only a few seconds, but it made a strong impact on fans (see Figures 1 and 2).

Fans quickly identified the location of the opening sequence and started to visit Washinomiya Shrine. According to Sakata Atsushi and Matsumoto Shinji (interview conducted 30 May 2008), two members of staff at the Commerce and Industry Association of Washimiya, most of the visitors immediately after the airing of the anime tended to visit the shrine surreptitiously, took pictures and left the shrine quietly.

About one month after the beginning of the airing of the anime, a self-published magazine (*dōjinshi*) *Lucky star TV animation version commemorative fan book: 'follow the sailor uniform'* was published on 4 May 2007 by an amateur writer called Izuki.[4] This was significant because it was published before any actions by the copyright holders or the locality. The magazine introduces the locations featured in the anime, including Washimiya, and mainly functions as a guidebook. 'The biggest reason was to avoid bothering the local residents', explained Izuki (interview conducted 21 February 2009) as he described his reasons for

Figure 1 The opening scene of the anime *Lucky star*. © Kagami YOSHIMIZU/Lucky Paradise

publishing the magazine such a short time after the beginning of the anime's broadcast. When he found out that there was a large online debate about where the *Lucky star* locations actually were, he became concerned that a large number of fans would start wandering around the town looking for them. 'To avoid criticism of the programme and prejudice against fans...I wanted to introduce the locations accurately to prevent fans getting lost during their visits.'

Figure 2 The anime *Lucky star*. © Kagami YOSHIMIZU/Lucky Paradise

The magazine contributed significantly to the formation of a positive relationship between fans and local residents by encouraging fans' pilgrimages to cause as little trouble as possible to local residents and by appealing to the fans' morals and consciences through their love for the anime. Following its initial publication, other versions have been published periodically.

Subsequently, the locations of the anime version of *Lucky star* were officially introduced by the copyright holders in the supplement 'Lucky Star style field trip booklet' (Rakisuta-teki ensoku no shiori) in the August 2007 issue of the anime magazine *Monthly Newtype* (published by Kadokawa). With this publication, Washimiya was introduced to a large number of fans, and there was a dramatic increase in the number of people visiting Washinomiya Shrine. It became a common sight at Washinomiya Shrine to see fans hanging up wooden votive plaques (*ema*) inscribed with drawings of anime characters and fans taking pictures of the shrine gate and the tea house Otori-chaya in the same composition as in the opening scene of the anime. The Commerce and Industry Association staff, which had not been aware of the anime until then, began to notice the *ema* plaques offering prayers or wishes that were 'completely different from traditional *ema*' (Kono anime ga sugoi! 2008, p. 30).

The Commerce and Industry Association contacts fans

On 19 July 2007, a posting was made on a website run by a resident of an area adjacent to Washimiya in Kuki city that read: 'Otaku [geeks/obsessive fans] are gathering at Washinomiya Shrine, and as a nearby resident, I'm worried about public safety.'[5] The Commerce and Industry Association of Washimiya was contacted by the *Sankei shinbun* newspaper, which wanted to confirm the circumstances surrounding this posting (Yamazaki 2008, p. 100). Following this incident, the Association began interviewing visitors to the shrine, and found out that a great number of fans were visiting because of *Lucky star* (Kono anime ga sugoi! 2008, p. 30; Matsumoto interview). Subsequently, the results of *Sankei shinbun*'s investigations were published on the Internet (*Sankei shinbun* 2007a, 2007b). As a result, not only fans but also those who read these articles became interested in seeing the fans' *ema* and began to visit the shrine as well.

As their interviews with fans progressed, communications increased between the fans and two young members of staff at the Commerce and Industry Association (Sakata and Matsumoto), who were conducting most of the interviews. Association staff began discussing how there were no souvenirs in Washimiya for fans travelling long distances to visit the town. Discussions about what could be done for fans led to suggestions such as selling souvenirs at the tea house Otori-chaya.

Meanwhile, Sakata found out about the self-published magazine by Izuki and contacted him directly. They discussed whether there would be a demand for mobile-phone straps sold as souvenirs. Following this initial contact, Izuki began, on a volunteer basis, to support events and product development projects initiated by the Association. The Association also began to ask fans their opinions whenever possible. They understood that they should not compromise on the quality of the events and products targeted at the fans. As a result, many fans like Izuki began to show up at the Association as volunteers and participated in brainstorming sessions. In addition, Sakata and Matsumoto also participated in a discussion on the social networking site 2 Channel, and asked for advice from fans via internet chat rooms (Yamazaki 2008, pp. 100–101).

Advice obtained through contact with fans in this manner led to the development of *omiyage*-style souvenir *manju* (steamed sweet buns) with the wording 'sacred site pilgrimage' (*junrei*) on the *manju*. When they began selling this product at the tea house Otori-chaya in boxes of six, they sold fifty boxes in a week. This trial selling of branded sweet buns convinced the staff of the Commerce and Industry Association that there was a demand for anime-related products and souvenirs. This led them to contact one of the copyright holders, Kadokawa (discussed in more detail below).

As demonstrated by the example of magazine author Izuki, spontaneous contributions to the locality were being made by fans of the anime who visited the site at this early stage of the tourism boom. The Commerce and Industry Association understood such gestures and took action to form a cooperative relationship. Many of those fans who interacted with the Association during this early period have continued to visit the Association's administrative office on a regular basis, chat with the staff and volunteer to help with the staging of events.

The Association, therefore, became the point of contact between the locality and fans. It identified itself with the fans' point of view, and created an atmosphere for a casual exchange of opinions. This approach greatly fostered the desire among fans to make a contribution to the community. With fans welcomed by the local community, many wanted to purchase goods produced locally by business operators who had embraced the anime that the fans adored. This sentiment became common among fans visiting Washimiya. In part due to media coverage of the approach taken by Washimiya and its link to regional development activities, fans often said how they wanted to contribute collectively to regional development as much as possible, even if what they could do individually was limited (various interviews with fans in Washimiya, 18–19 July 2009).

The Commerce and Industry Association's structure and formula for collaboration with fans

There are five full-time members of staff at the Commerce and Industry Association of Washimiya, and Sakata and Matsumoto (in their 30s at the time) have been in charge of *Lucky star* tie-in projects from the beginning. They believe that the small scale of the project enabled flexible, timely action. Matsumoto commented:

We will miss the boat if we follow the local government approach to annual budgets and project plans, which first establishes a budget and then starts projects the following year. We can produce big results because we ignore these things and initiate projects at the right time. The size and structure of the Commerce and Industry Association of Washimiya Town allow us to do this.

(Matsumoto Shinji, interview conducted 30 May 2008)

Also significant is the role of the Association's president, who assigned this large project to these two energetic young members of staff and then backed them up at all times by saying, 'don't be afraid of failure. I'll take full responsibility' (*Mainichi shinbun* 2008). Sakata and Matsumoto acknowledge that they were able to achieve as much as they did only because of the Association president's stance (Yamazaki 2008, p. 102).

On the other hand, the small scale of the Commerce and Industry Association can be a disadvantage when holding events. However, as mentioned above, in Washimiya fans participated as volunteers in product development meetings and events and made up the numbers by acting as advisors and support staff. There have been about five to six volunteer members who have participated continuously from an early stage, and about fifteen volunteers have helped out during events. The Commerce and Industry Association believes that, because of such arrangements, 'it was possible to accurately grasp the needs of the fans and that led to a sense of unity with the fans' (Commerce and Industry Association 2008).

Many of these early-stage volunteers had experience taking part in Comiket (Comic market), the largest self-published comic book fair in the world, which is held twice a year in Tokyo. It has been suggested that their voluntary actions relate to the volunteering culture of Comiket.

Contact between local residents and fans

The Association organized a 'stamp rally' with the participation of shops serving food and drinks from April to September 2008. In this project, each of the twelve participating shops served one special item related to one anime character. If participants purchased all the items, they received an original item as a reward. Many fans walked around the town visiting these twelve shops, which were located throughout the town. The number of fans that purchased all the items during the approximately six-month period of the event reached 624 (Commerce and Industry Association 2008). Through this project, anime fans were no longer interacting only with the Association. Their interaction with local residents increased, and some even became fans of a particular shop, too.

So contact between fans and local residents increased. The person in charge of the local traditional festival, Haji-sai, invited fans to join the festival as well. With the cooperation of the local community, fans made their own *mikoshi* (portable Shinto Shrine) decorated with anime characters (Okamoto 2011). The *Lucky*

Figure 3 The *Lucky star mikoshi* (left) and the traditional *mikoshi* (portable shrine, right) at Haji Festival. Photograph courtesy of the Washimiya Town Commerce and Industry Association, September 2010.

star mikoshi has been seen at the festival every year since its first appearance in September 2008. It has become an annual event at which more than 120 anime fans come to the town from all over Japan to shoulder the *mikoshi* and walk around the town (Matsumoto Shinji, interview conducted 31 March 2011; see Figure 3). The *Lucky star mikoshi* gained even greater international attention when it was paraded through the Asia Square during Japan Day at Expo 2010 in Shanghai at the request of CoFesta (Japan International Contents Festival), which is organized by the Ministry of Economy, Trade and Industry (Figure 4). Local people from Washimiya and Japanese anime fans travelled to Shanghai to carry the *mikoshi*.

Summary

In the early stages, when fans were visiting the site as pioneers (see the article by Okamoto Takeshi in this issue), a conscientious fan showed concern for the locality by producing a guidebook so that fans could avoid causing problems. The local Commerce and Industry Association responded by identifying themselves with the fans and strived to make contact in various ways, such as through asking advice from fans. Through deepening mutual understanding of each

Figure 4 The *Lucky star mikoshi* being paraded at Shanghai Expo 2010. Photograph courtesy of the Washimiya Town Commerce and Industry Association, September 2010.

other's situations and needs, and through contact between the locality and fans, a cooperative locality–fans relationship was formed.

As described in the introduction to this article, discussions of contents tourism have focused on regional development achieved through localities collaborating with copyright holders, while little attention has been paid to spontaneous actions by fans. One of the unique characteristics of the Washimiya case is the collaborative relationship formed through the spontaneous actions of fans and the adoption of fans' perspectives by the locality.

Formation of the relationship between the copyright holders and the locality

The most important issue the locality must pay attention to when forming a cooperative relationship with anime production companies is the handling of copyrights. In recent years the control of copyrights has become extremely strict, especially in relation to holding events and creating products using anime characters.

The copyright holders for the original manga version of *Lucky star* are the author Yoshimizu Kagami and Kadokawa. For the anime version they are

Yoshimizu Kagami and Lucky Paradise, the production committee of the anime which comprises various investors including Kadokawa. In both cases, Kadokawa was the contact for copyright usage by a third party. All correspondence concerning copyrights in the case of the Commerce and Industry Association of Washimiya have been handled solely by Kadokawa.

As described above, the Association staff collecting information on *Lucky star* contacted Kadokawa in September 2007 saying that they wanted to develop an anime-related product that could be sold as a souvenir of Washimiya. In response, they were asked to make a proposal (Yamazaki 2008, p. 101). Both Sakata and Matsumoto prepared as many proposals as possible, and in October they and the Vice President of the Commerce and Industry Association visited the headquarters of Kadokawa. At this meeting, they heard a counter-proposal to hold a Kadokawa-planned event targeting fans that combined a visit to Washinomiya Shrine and a brunch at the tea house Otori-chaya.

The Association viewed this development as an opportunity, and quickly contacted all the actors involved – in particular Washinomiya Shrine – to get them to accept the proposal. In early November they were contacted by Kadokawa, which had fixed the schedules of the voice actors who, it was planned, would participate in the event. The proposed date was 2 December. Though the Association had another event planned on that day, they concluded that this was their one and only chance to hold such an event given the complexity of the business operation, and so the decision was made to hold the event on the proposed date (Sakata and Matsumoto, interview).

The plans for the production and sale of an original anime-related Washimiya souvenir were brought forward as well. Based on discussions with those fans who had volunteered to provide advice on product development, the Association planned the development of a mobile-phone strap in the shape of a small *ema*, made of paulownia wood and decorated with *Lucky star* characters. Together with the various companies involved in the anime production committee, Kadokawa responded to the Association's proposal as flexibly as possible, including in relation to the usage of copyrights, because they considered it to be 'a cooperative effort for vitalizing the town' and 'promotion and advertisement' for the anime (Kadokawa interview 22 December 2010).

Usually the point of contact for collaboration with localities for production companies like Kadokawa is either the department/person in charge of sales and promotion or the department/person in charge of copyrights. In the case of Washimiya and *Lucky star*, Kadokawa understood the importance of regional development, so until regional development got under way the sales promotion section acted as the contact and handled copyrights. Thus, the project did not end up as a mere character business, with Kadokawa insisting rigidly on fees for the use of its copyrights, but developed into a model of 'regional development + sales promotion' where Kadokawa was happy to loosen its copyright fees structure for the sake of Washimiya's development plans and increased publicity and sales for Kadokawa's publications.

Holding events

In this way, the staging of events and the production and sale of anime-related products began.

On 2 December 2007, a '*Lucky Star* Brunch and official shrine visit in Washimiya' was held at the tea house Otori-chaya and Washinomiya Shrine. This event was planned by the anime production committee, Lucky Paradise, organized by the youth group of the Commerce and Industry Association and attended by three voice actresses, a voice actor and the writer Yoshimizu. Also, about ten fans volunteered on the day of the event to help with crowd control and other tasks.

The event began with lunch at Otori-chaya, which served a special meal prepared for the fans. The three voice actresses and the voice actor helped with serving the meal and operating the register. Following lunch, guided by the two actresses who voiced the Hiiragi sisters and the other voice actress and actor, the fans visited Washinomiya Shrine. According to the Commerce and Industry Association, 3,500 people participated in this event (Sakata and Matsumoto, interview 30 May 2008).

The event was a great success, and, according to the Association, there were only one or two complaints from local residents. Most of the Association and related organizations' staff and residents got the impression that the fans were courteous and had good manners (*Mainichi shinbun* 2008). Washinomiya Shrine is visited by about 100,000 people annually for *hatsumōde* (New Year's Shrine visit) and is also visited by a large number of people during its festivals, but the residents were quite surprised that the participants in this event had such good manners compared to the usual visitors to Washinomiya Shrine. Furthermore, the event was covered extremely favourably by the media, including NHK (Japan's public broadcaster), and the manners of fans got even better in response to such coverage. According to local sources, this forming of positive public opinion greatly stimulated the subsequent development of the project (Matsumoto, interview 30 May 2008). This point not only served to elevate the public image of the anime, but also publicized the high level of social contribution being made by Kadokawa and the anime production committee.

Development of anime-related products

The Commerce and Industry Association commissioned the production of the mobile-phone strap (mentioned above) from Iijima Paulownia Chest Factory which was operated by the President of the local Traditional Craftsmen

Association of the local traditional craft: Kasukabe paulownia wood dressing (*Yomiuri shinbun* 2007; mobile-phone strap publicity literature).

Following this order, a total of eleven designs were completed and it was decided to sell the straps at a unit price of 630 yen. However, when they first approached member shops of the Association to sell the product, hardly any shops were interested. The Association was finally able to persuade seventeen shops, but only by guaranteeing that the shops would not be responsible for any losses and all unsold products would be collected by the Association at its own expense (Yamazaki 2008, p. 101; Matsumoto, interview).

However, at the event held for the fans on 2 December, the Association sold their entire stock of 2,200 straps in one day at a special tent they set up for the event. On the next day, even with the sales targeted at the general public at the seventeen participating shops, the total stock of 1,000 straps that had been distributed to the seventeen shops was all sold within thirty minutes of the opening of each shop. This led to forty-three shops participating in the second sales period that began on 20 December, and sixty shops participating in the third sales period that began on 10 February. Furthermore, a total of 3,000 straps distributed among the forty-three participating shops (sold within an hour of opening at all forty-three shops) and a total of 8,500 straps distributed to the sixty participating shops (sold within an hour of opening at the shops located in the shrine avenue shopping district, and sold within about a week in all of the other shops located in other areas) were sold in the second and third sales periods respectively (Commerce and Industry Association data).

Actions taken by the locality out of consideration for the copyright holders

Appreciative of Kadokawa's cooperation with Washimiya's regional development and the fact that Kadokawa was a commercial enterprise, the Commerce and Industry Association wanted to develop a win–win relationship. In order to do so, they considered it important to understand and respect the anime. Consequently, they worked to achieve various aims through holding events and selling anime-related products: these included enhancing the images of the original manga and anime, stimulating the development of tie-ins and increasing the sales of Kadokawa's publications. The Commerce and Industry Association contributed to increasing the sales of Kadokawa magazine *Comptiq*, which runs the manga version of *Lucky star*, by supplying straps as free gifts for readers (Commerce and Industry Association 2008). 'If we are successful in contributing to the sales of the magazine, we are able to pay back Kadokawa Shoten Publishing for all that they have done for us so far', said a member of staff involved in this project at the Commerce and Industry Association (Sakata, interview 28 May 2011).

Mutual benefit through the 'regional development + sales promotion' model

Based on the discussion so far, it is clear that there were three significant points in the formation of a beneficial relationship between the Commerce and Industry Association of Washimiya and Kadokawa.

First, due to the decision made by the copyright holders to make staff in charge of sales promotion the contact people, the two parties were able to form a cooperative relationship that benefited both sides. This was a result of the altruism of both parties, such as the efforts made to contribute to the sales of the manga/anime and magazines on the part of the locality and the efforts to contribute to regional development on the part of the copyright holders. They were able to conduct successful business based on this philosophy. This was made possible largely because those involved in the project on both sides made an effort to ensure there would be mutual benefits and to form good relationships at a staff level. With the events and sales of anime-related products in Washimiya on a stable footing given the collaborative relationship that had built up, the contact on the Kadokawa side was moved to the copyright holders section of the company in April 2008. The existence of the positive relationship today would not have been possible without the positive basis on which relationship developed from the outset.

Second, because of the single contact on the production side, processing the complicated anime copyright procedures was done smoothly. It is necessary to understand Japanese anime production methods in recent years in order to understand the complicated anime copyrights processes. Anime are typically produced by a 'production committee'. A company with a planned production solicits investment from a number of other companies, and then a production committee is formed by those companies that choose to invest. In the case of *Lucky star*, Lucky Paradise is the production committee. In most cases, the anime copyrights are held by the writer and the production committee. Usually profits are distributed among the production committee members in proportion to the size of their investment. Consequently, the writer of the original manga and the anime may be the same, but copyright holders usually differ between the two media.

When a locality contacts copyright holders, usually the contact for a manga is the publisher and the contact for an anime is the section in charge of either sales promotion or copyrights of one of the companies that belongs to the production committee. Especially in the case of an anime production committee, the handling and negotiation of copyrights becomes complicated because the committee is made up of several companies. In the case of *Lucky star*, however, it was possible for Kadokawa to be the sole contact and conduct negotiations because it was the publisher of the original manga and a member of the anime production committee. This point was crucial at an administrative level for enabling extremely smooth negotiations between the locality and the copyright holders.

Finally, a positive relationship was formed between the two parties (locality and production committee) at an interpersonal level. According to my interviews conducted in Washimiya, the relation was portrayed as not merely a business relationship, but as a relationship based on warm ties between the various sides. Continuity in personnel and the maintenance of those close contacts have also been extremely beneficial. Most of the local people who were actually involved in the collaborative projects with the copyright holders were individual business owners and local volunteers who normally would have nothing to do with copyrights. Furthermore, even though in this case there was a production committee, the staff representing the copyright holders were experienced in handling copyrights and thus could set out rules for the handling of copyrights with little difficulty according to the ratio of investments. If the contacts are not set up clearly, the prospects for collaboration can fall through no matter how dedicated the local people are as they get bounced around from one contact to another due to the complex rights.

In addition to setting up visible contact, the staff on both sides contacted each other frequently and each was constantly acting with the other's benefit in mind. The locality was keen not to do anything that would not benefit the anime or would damage the image of the original manga/anime. Likewise the copyright holders were keen to avoid actions that would not benefit the locality. These mutually supportive stances resulted in the enhancement of the 'added value' (brand power) for both the locality and the manga/anime through the events that were organized and the development of anime-related products.

Conclusions and implications

This article has analysed the development of contents tourism in Washimiya from the standpoints of the relationships formed between the locality and the fans and between the locality and the copyright holders. Both relationships were formed with consideration for the other and by carefully building the relationships on an interpersonal level. In other words, each relationship was based on consideration for the other, even if it sometimes led to a superficial loss for one of the sides. The result was a strong spirit of cooperation.

Not all relationships are as smooth. In some other cases, fans have caused trouble for local communities or visiting fans have not been welcomed by the local communities. For example, *Silver spoon* is an anime first broadcast on television in July 2013. It is about school life in an agricultural facility in the Tokachi-Obihiro region of Hokkaido. Fears that visiting fans would spread diseases in livestock caused the production company to ask fans in the closing credits to refrain from visiting the area and the facility on which the story is modelled.

In another example, *Ichigo Mashimaro*, which was broadcast from July to October 2005, depicted the everyday life of a group of young girls in a residential area of Hamamatsu city, Shizuoka prefecture. As in the case of Washimiya, fans began to visit this area following the airing of the show. However, there was an incident in which the police questioned a fan acting suspiciously in the vicinity of a school that appeared in the story. Thereafter, a notice was printed in the magazine that regularly publishes the original serialized manga asking fans to 'refrain from such behaviour' because visiting fans were causing trouble for the local residents (Barasuii 2006, p. 179).

As can be seen, problems between fans and local residents can easily occur when fans begin to visit the sites on a 'pilgrimage to a sacred place' in the anime because the facilities or areas are not prepared for visits by tourists. Even in the Washimiya case, while the shrine, the centre of the 'pilgrimage', was by nature a facility managed on the assumption that it would be visited by the general public, it was situated in a residential area and there were times when the media reported concerns about worsening security caused by fan visits. However, in the Washimiya case, these issues were overcome because all the parties showed consideration to the circumstances of others and were able to build positive relationships as a result. In fact, while there are numerous anime shows that have been produced which are set in an actual location, there are only a few cases in which such positive relationships have been built. Even among these cases, the Washimiya case is exceptional in that the various parties have maintained long-standing, positive and strong relationships.

Furthermore, it is particularly noteworthy that communication was fostered because the anime contents – *Lucky star* – acted as a mediator. As is clear from the comments of fans and staff of the Commerce and Industry Association, everybody involved in the project had an unwavering belief that the most important thing was the anime, namely the contents themselves.

This point – that mutual understanding and consideration emerged among the various actors because of their shared respect and adoration for the contents – is significant. If contents tourism is to be viewed not just as business pertaining to licenses or economic transactions between host and guest, but instead as communication between people in an actual space and time with contents at the centre of those interactions, then this constitutes a vital insight into what conditions might enable successful contents tourism elsewhere.

When this point is applied to the actors in the contents tourism model developed by Horiuchi (2010), an even more dynamic model is developed (see Figure 5).

Such conclusions may sound highly conventional. However, having become an advanced economy and competitive society that places the highest priority on economic profit, the reality in Japan today is that economic relationships based on consideration for others have become rarer or more difficult in economic circles. What the Washimiya case demonstrates so convincingly is that consideration of others in itself may be the basis for good business. This was the secret of Washimiya's success and created a local shopping district where loyalty and compassion still exist.

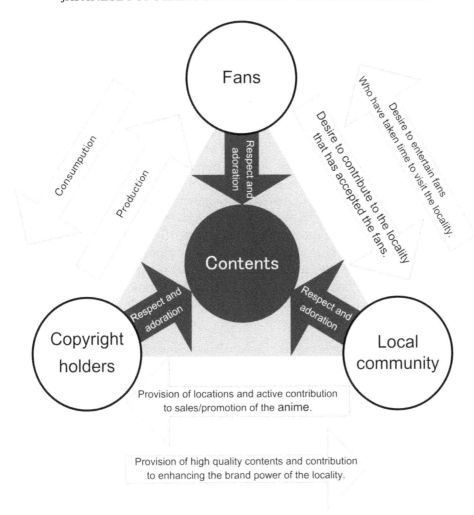

Figure 5 The players in contents tourism, based on Horiuchi (2010, p. 62) and revised by the author.

These conclusions suggest a number of strategies for the realization of successful contents tourism.

Local community and fans

The locality decided to treat the fans without prejudice. Rather than being otaku (geeks, or anime fans viewed in perhaps a condescending way), they were important guests who used their precious time to come to Washimiya. As such, the locality considered how to make their visits to Washimiya as enjoyable as possible.

Furthermore, the locality remained uncompromising on the quality of the events and anime-related products. They came to understand the importance of the anime to the fans through constantly approaching them for advice on event projects and product development. This allowed the fans to bring the anime into their lives in a very real way and greatly enhanced the satisfaction of the fans.

On the other hand, partly due to the influence of conscientious fans from an early stage, many fans were conscious of not causing trouble to local residents. Many came to feel it would be rude to just visit the site and leave immediately afterwards, and many felt that they wanted to give back something to the community that had welcomed them. Fans were warmly accepted by local residents precisely because of such attitudes. Strong bonds developed between fans and the residents, as illustrated by the participation of fans in the local festival. Such attitudes on the part of fans were extremely beneficial to the relationship.

As the relationship has developed, more fans have recognized that shopping at local small businesses is the most direct way to contribute to the local economy. Through patronage of local shops, even though their purchases may be small, it became common among the fans to shop with a feeling of gratitude towards the local business operators who accepted them and the anime they love.[6] Developing such relationships and attitudes constitutes a powerful force to vitalize localities economically.

Local community and copyright holders

While moving forward with the tie-in with *Lucky star*, the Commerce and Industry Association of Washimiya paid respect to the original contents so that their activities would be beneficial for the anime (namely, they avoided damaging the reputation of the anime and tried to contribute to enhancing its image). In other words, they aimed for a high-quality secondary use, whereby the contents could be used for further product development and sales.

As already mentioned, this approach was taken partially with the aim of developing products and events that accommodated the needs of the fans. However, the other important aim was to give maximum consideration to the copyright holders' commercial interests. The association, therefore, was not just thinking about promoting local industries and tourism.

On the other hand, increasing the commercial spin-offs from *Lucky star* was a part of Kadokawa's sales strategy, so the copyright holders provided maximum flexibility in terms of copyright usage by the locality. The copyright holders understood well that the enlargement of a secondary market at the locality would provide opportunities for the general public and travellers to come into contact with information on the anime (information regarding the original contents), and that would have the effect of increasing interest in *Lucky star*.

The significant point here is that, due to such mutual consideration, the locality actively contributed to fostering promotion and sales of the anime and the production side contributed to enhancing the contents tourism and brand power of the locality. Thus the two were able to form a complementary relationship.

But other copyright holders have different attitudes towards local communities intending to incorporate their animation into local tourist attractions. There have been only a few cases in which, as in the case of Washimiya, copyright holders and the local community have maintained a relationship where both of them highly respect the interests of the other.

For example, the anime *K-On! (Keion!)*, which was broadcast from April 2009, was set in Toyosato town in Shiga prefecture. This led many of its fans to visit the town. Fans and the local community proposed various promotional activities to the copyright holders in an attempt to attract more tourists into the town. However, the copyright holders did not agree to recognize the town as the place where the animation was set. Nor have they expressed willingness to get directly involved in the proposed activities with the fans and the community (Okamoto 2012). This situation has not changed as this article goes to press (July 2014) and is another indication of just how successful the Washimiya case has been.

Another key lesson from the Washimiya case is that two phrases which are often confused, 'contents tourism' and 'character business', are not synonymous. Many contents tourism cases have led to the development of tie-in products utilizing characters from anime. In this sense, on many occasions contents tourism does indeed overlap with the character business. However, the sale of such character products is only a single element in the context of tourism. More precisely, when considering contents tourism, not only the character business but also many other phenomena must be considered in relation to the copyright holders, localities and fans. Also, the character business as a part of contents tourism has different aims from the character business in which product development is the work of a single company. The character business engaged in by a single company is developed within the context of the company's management strategies, and the critical issue is to increase the number of fans of the character and improve sales. However, the character business within the context of contents tourism needs to be developed collaboratively with the copyright holders and the locality aiming at regional development (meaning that a locality benefits economically, socially and culturally). The important task, therefore, is to make the character fans into fans of the locality as well.

In conclusion, the Washimiya case raises important lessons for local governments forming contents tourism policies.

The pursuit of profit at the expense of constructive, collaborative relationships became rampant in Japan during the period of rapid economic growth and the bubble economy. However, in the midst of the economic stagnation since the 1990s, the Washimiya case suggests we can rediscover that business is essentially a 'lasting relationship' between people, whether between local societies and copyright holders or between the sellers (hosts) and the buyers (guests).

It can be argued that this is common sense. However, in the neoliberal world order, people in Japan and across the globe have often overlooked such common sense. The fact that one of the triggers for such re-discovery of humanistic basics was an anime attests to one of the many charms of Japanese anime and its social significance beyond simply being light entertainment or pop culture.

As mentioned at the beginning of the article, there has recently been a lot of discussion regarding contents tourism in Japan, especially by the government. However, the arguments in this article relating to the broader implications of contents tourism for Japanese society and social values have never been raised in such discussions. Discussions on contents tourism are still at an early stage, and hardly any research has been conducted on cases other than Washimiya. The framework for contents tourism research must be developed promptly through further research and comparative analyses of various approaches.

Notes

1. Washimiya town merged with Kuki city on 23 March 2010. In this article, I use 'Washimiya' to indicate the territory of the former Washimiya Town.
2. Washimiya is in the northeast of the prefecture and roughly in the centre of the Kanto Plain (approximately 50 kilometres north of Tokyo). The total area of the town was 1,390 hectares before its municipal merger into Kuki city. The town has two stations: Higashi Washinomiya station on the JR Utsunomiya line and Washinomiya station on the Tobu Isesaki line. It takes approximately one hour from the town to central Tokyo.
3. For example, 'Possibilities of Location Tourism in Animations – Pilgrimage and Tourism Resources', Japan Location Market Symposium at the Tokyo International Anime Fair hosted by the Ministry of Economy, Trade and Industry and UNIJAPAN (18 March 2009); 'Public Meeting on Inbound Promotions and Other Methods Utilizing Animation Contents', an Affiliated Forum of the 'Tokyo International Anime Fair 2010' hosted by the Japan Tourism Agency (25 March 2010).
4. Izuki is his pen name, by which all his publications are known. His real name is Osakabe Keitarō.
5. Otaku ga atsumaru Washinomiya jinja. Available from: http://kuki-shimin.com/archives/219 [Accessed 6 June 2008].
6. I conduct field surveys on a regular basis and was able to hear these kinds of remarks from fans and several shopkeepers.

References

Barasuii, 2006. Ichigo Mashimaro. *Gekkan comic dengekidaio*, March edn. Tokyo: MediaWorks, 172–179.
Chiteki zaisan senryaku honbu, 2004. Chiteki zaisan suishin keikaku 2004. Available from: http://www.kantei.go.jp/jp/singi/titeki2/kettei/040527f.pdf [Accessed 12 June 2014].
Commerce and Industry Association of Washimiya Town, 2008. Chiiki kasseika purojekuto 'Rakisuta' taiappu jigyō. Unpublished Washimiya town documents, March 2008.
Horiuchi, J., 2010. Rekishi kontentsu no juyō ni kansuru jittai chōsa: 'Shinsengumi' kontentsu ni kansuru chōsa hōkoku. *In: Proceedings of the Kontentsu bunkashi taikai Conference 2010*. Yamagata: Kontentsu Bunkashi Gakkai, 61–71.
Izuki, 2007. *Rakisuta TV animeka kinen FanBook 'Okkake! Sērāfuku*. Self-published manga (*dōjinshi*).
Kono anime ga sugoi! Henshūbu, ed., 2008. *Kono anime ga sugoi! 2008*. Tokyo: Takarajimasha.

Lucky star website, 2007a. Rakisuta no buranchi & kōshiki sanpai in Washinomiya, Kokuchi pēji. Available from: http://www.lucky-ch.com/info/info_washinomiya.html [Accessed 12 June 2014].

Lucky star website 2007b. Rakisuta no buranchi & kōshiki sanpai in Washinomiya. Ibento repōto. Available from: http://www.lucky-ch.com/info/info_event_071202.html [Accessed 12 June 2014].

Mainichi shinbun, 2008. Hito, Saitama: ninki anime de machi okoshi wo suru Saitō Masaru, Washinomiya-machi shōkō kaichō. *Mainichi shinbun* (Saitama edition), 1 May, p. 24.

Masubuchi, T., 2010. *Monogatari wo tabi suru hitobito: kontentsu tsūrizumu to wa nani ka.* Tokyo: Sairyusha.

Ministry of Land, Infrastructure, Transport and Tourism, the Ministry of Economy, Trade and Industry, and the Agency for Cultural Affairs, 2005. Eizō tō kontentsu no sakusei, katsuyō ni yoru chiiki shinkō no arikata ni kansuru chōsa hōkokusho. Available from: http://www.mlit.go.jp/kokudokeikaku/souhatu/h16seika/12eizou/12eizou.htm [Accessed 12 June 2014].

Okamoto, T., 2010. Kontentsu indyūsuto tsūrizumu: kontentsu kara kangaeru jōhō shakai no ryokō kōdō. *Kontentsu bunkashi kenkyū*, 3, 48–68.

Okamoto, T., 2011. Kontentsu tsūrizumu ni okeru hosupitariti manejimento: Haji-sai 'Rakisuta mikoshi' wo jirei to shite. *Hospitality*, 18, 165–174.

Okamoto, T. 2012. Ryokōshashudō-gata kontentsu tsūrizumu ni okeru kankōshigen management: 'Rakisuta' seichi 'Washimiya' to 'Keion!' seichi 'Toyosato' no hikakukara. *Nihon jōhōkeiei gakkaishi*, 32 (3), 59–71.

Saitama Prefecture, 2009. Hōdō happyō shiryō: Dai 1 kai 'Saitama ken anime tourism kentō iinkai' no kaisai kekka ni tsuite. Saitama-ken sangyō rōdōbu kankōka, 23 June.

Sankei shinbun, 2007a. Kantō saiko no jinja ni ani-ota sattō, jimoto konwaku, ishoku no ema mo. *Sankei shinbun*, 25 June. Available from: http://sankei.jp.msn.com/entertainments/game/070725/gam0707252202005-n1.htm [Accessed 4 June 2008].

Sankei shinbun, 2007b. Kantō saiko no jinja ni 'rakisuta' otaku sattō, jimoto 'chian no mondai ga'. *Sankei shinbun*, 25 July. Available from: http://headlines.yahoo.co.jp/hl?a=20070725-00000925-san-soci [accessed July 28, 2007].

Uno, T., 2011. *Ritoru pūpuru no jidai.* Tokyo: Gentōsha.

Yamamura, T., 2008. Anime seichi no seiritsu to sono tenkai ni kansuru kenkyū: anime sakuhin 'Rakisuta' ni yoru Saitama-ken Washimiya-machi no ryokyaku yūchi ni kansuru ichikōsai. *Kokusai Kōhō Media, Kankōgaku jānaru*, 7, 145–164.

Yamamura, T., 2011a. 'Anime de machizukuri' kara 'anime to machizukuri' he. *Saitama shinbun Saitamania*, 31 Dec., p. 2.

Yamamura, T., 2011b. *Manga, anime de chiiki shinkō.* Tokyo: Tokyo Hōrei Shuppan.

Yamamura, T., 2012. Shuku 'kamisama hajimemashita' animeka. *Saitama shinbun Saitamania*, 20 Oct., p. 2.

Yamazaki, M., 2008. Moe anime de machi okoshi!? Washimiya-machi Shōkōkai ni kyōmi shinshin. *ascii*, July, pp. 98–102.

Yomiuri shinbun, 2007. Anime ema de machiokoshi no kigan 'Rakisuta' keitai sutorappu, Washinomiya de hanbai he. *Yomiuri shinbun* (Tokyo edn), 10 Nov., p. 33.

Yamamura Takayoshi is a professor in the Center for Advanced Tourism Studies, Hokkaido University, Japan. His main research interests are cultural tourism planning and media design, cultural resource management and heritage tourism studies. He is the author of *Community development through anime and manga* (Anime, manga de chiiki shinkō, Tokyo Hōrei Shuppan) and numerous articles on heritage and pop culture tourism.

Taiga dramas and tourism: historical contents as sustainable tourist resources

PHILIP SEATON

Abstract: Taiga dramas are one of the flagship events of the Japanese television year. These historical drama series, broadcast on NHK General over the course of a year in Sunday evening prime time, have induced large-scale tourism to sites related to the events depicted in the dramas. This article investigates the scopes and natures of the tourism booms induced by two dramas set in the Bakumatsu (1853–1868) period: *Shinsengumi!* in 2004 and *Ryōma-den* in 2010. Analysis of the impacts these dramas had in Hakodate, Kōchi, Hino and Kyoto reveals the complex dynamics of heritage tourism generated by NHK's dramas. In addition to the narrative qualities of the drama, the scale and nature of the tourism boom are determined by factors such as prevailing economic conditions and the infrastructure capabilities of regions/ locations to cash in on the influx of tourists. The predictable, annual tourism boom induced by NHK's dramas makes the series an important case study within the broader field of film-induced tourism.

Introduction

On 22 June 2011, NHK announced that its Taiga drama for 2013, *Yae no Sakura*, would tell the story of Niijima Yae. Niijima took part in the defence of Aizu-Wakamatsu Castle (in modern-day Fukushima prefecture) during the Boshin War (1868–1869) and was dubbed the 'Bakumatsu Joan of Arc'.[1] NHK had not originally planned to make Niijima the heroine of the drama series for 2013, but, following the 11 March 2011 triple disaster, there had been voices within NHK saying that the choice of drama should somehow contribute to recovery. Chief producer Naitō Shinsuke commented, 'Following the Tohoku Earthquake, we wanted a story that would depict the soul and bonds of the Japanese people. We also hope it will encourage the disaster-affected areas' (*Hokkaidō shinbun* 2011b).

'Encouragement' did not simply refer to moral support, akin to the broader Ganbarō Nippon (Do your best Japan) campaign following 3/11. NHK clearly aimed to provide a financial boost in the form of a tourism boom to an area reeling from the Fukushima Daiichi Nuclear Power Plant disaster. Almost immediately, Aizu-Wakamatsu city established a 'Taiga Drama' project team. It was announced that a museum would be created to house costumes used during the drama and other memorabilia. Projected visitor numbers, based on estimates from increases in tourist numbers at locations of Taiga dramas in previous years, were around 600,000 (Fukushima Minpō 2012). In February 2012, a website (http://www.yae-mottoshiritai.jp/) about Niijima produced by the Aizu-Wakamatsu tourism association went online. And the Fukushima tourism association used NHK's announcement to launch a tourism promotional campaign at events such as the Sapporo Snow Festival, at which one of the gigantic snow statues was a replica of Aizu-Wakamatsu Castle.

Such activities reveal the contemporary received wisdom in Japan that the locations featured in the year's Taiga drama are going to receive a massive influx of additional tourists. Tourism drives, with all the associated merchandizing, are now standard operating procedure for local tourism authorities and regional development agencies when the Taiga drama comes to town. This article explores the phenomenon of tourism induced by NHK's Taiga dramas (hereafter 'drama-induced tourism'). It focuses on drama-induced tourism during 2004 and 2010 resulting from the NHK Taiga dramas *Shinsengumi!* and *Ryōma-den*.

Taiga dramas as tourism inducers

Predicting whether a film or drama will be a hit with the general public is notoriously difficult. Predicting whether a film or drama can then go on to engender sufficient levels of tourist activity for promoters to invest in tourism tie-ins is even more difficult. Yet, in Japan it is routinely assumed that Taiga dramas will induce tourism booms, and local authorities in the locations used for the drama initiate tourism promotion plans on the basis of that assumption.

Broadly speaking, there are two main reasons why Taiga dramas routinely induce large-scale tourism: the scale and impact of the drama creates a massive pool of potential tourists, and the nature of the contents makes it meaningful and possible for fans to extend their enjoyment of the drama via tourism.

Taiga dramas (literally 'Grand River' dramas) have been an institution on Japanese television since the first series in 1963 (the series *Gō, himetachi no sengoku* broadcast throughout 2011 was the fiftieth series; see NHK 2011). The drama is a sweeping historical character study focusing on a main hero/heroine. The series typically runs for an entire year (forty to fifty weekly episodes). Sustained attention over such a period of time maximizes the numbers of people who come into contact with the drama. The status of Taiga dramas as arguably *the* flagship event of the Japanese television drama year means that the subject matter of the next drama series is announced to national fanfare, and the actor or actress in the leading role is instantly catapulted to national fame. Such a massive cultural event inevitably precipitates many spin-off products and events, which further enhance the scale and reach of the drama's contents.

Broadcast at prime time on Sunday evenings (8 pm), Taiga dramas typically gain high viewing figures. Data from Video Data Research (2012) indicate that average ratings for each series were in the 16–24 per cent range between 1997 and 2011. These figures are impressive given the hundreds of other competing channels in the satellite/digital age. Before the explosion in the number of channels in the 1990s, even higher viewing figures for Taiga dramas (in the 25–35 per cent range) were standard. Given Japan's population of 126 million, such data represent a potential pool of drama-induced tourists in the tens of millions.

The second reason why Taiga dramas induce significant levels of tourism is that interest in the subject matter may easily be deepened through tourist behaviour. Taiga dramas are almost always set in the pre-modern period (up to and including the Bakumatsu period, 1853–1868), which is an immensely popular period of Japanese history depicted in numerous other *jidaigeki* (period dramas) produced for both cinema and television (see Standish 2005). Also significant in the context of tourism creation is the specificity of the location that should be visited by drama fans. The heroes/heroines featured in Taiga dramas tend to be already famous national figures, so the settings of the stories typically contain pre-existing sites (museums, temples, graves, battlefields and so on), which constitute the basic tourist itinerary for fans. The heroes/heroines typically have strong connections to a particular *han* (domain) from the feudal era, and that becomes the focus of tourist activity.

Furthermore, tourism inducement is woven into the drama itself. It is standard practice these days (and was so for both dramas studied in this article) for there to be a short documentary section of a couple of minutes at the end of each episode that tells viewers about sites related to the events depicted that week, including instructions on how to reach them on public transport. Over the course of the series, Taiga dramas will provide a total of roughly two hours of direct advertising for the historical sites featured in the drama.

Taiga dramas, therefore, do not create tourism to locations where there was no tourism before. They boost visitation to existing sites within the heritage tourism sector, although some localities may add to their tourism assets in expectation of the tourism rush precipitated by the drama. Indeed, the heroes and heroines of Taiga dramas have typically featured in many other dramas, so there is a cumulative effect over a period of many years in which localities build up a set of heritage/cultural tourist assets relating to local heroes/stories that are (re)visited when the Taiga drama features those contents. Taiga dramas, therefore, fit into a broader context of multi-use: the historical contents feature in many media forms and are promoted by local tourism authorities/sectors in the form of museums, monuments and merchandise.

Consequently, historical contents are recognized and treated as invaluable, sustainable tourist resources by localities. They are ideal for multi-use (the same contents in various formats: fiction/non-fiction, anime/live action, manga/printed word, computer games, museums and so on). There are no copyright issues for stories and heroes dating back a century or more in contrast to the considerable copyright restrictions regarding contemporary contents (see the article by Yamamura Takayoshi in this issue). Furthermore, the nature of historical narratives is that they may be constantly updated to resonate with the needs and priorities of the times. As such, on top of multi-use there is extensive re-narration and recycling over time. Popular historical contents such as the Shinsengumi and Sakamoto Ryōma stories have been the subject of many remakes over the years.

The combination of all these factors makes Taiga dramas powerful inducers of tourism. Other individual drama series (such as the well-known example of *Winter sonata*) may have led to similar or greater levels of tourism, but these are one-off cases and not the predictable annual event that is the tourism boom induced by NHK's Taiga drama series.

Economic impact

The regularity and predictability of drama-induced tourism have made the local economic impacts of the dramas via tourism a standard part of the discourse surrounding the drama. NHK's commemorative book to mark the fiftieth series of the genre included a section about areas in Japan that have experienced tourism booms, and profiles some of the spin-off products and tourist sites related to the dramas (2011, pp. 190–207).

Local branches of the Bank of Japan now regularly forecast the economic impact of the tourism induced by the drama. The forecasts are released in advance of the drama, but the estimates for both dramas featured in this article were revised upwards after the drama was over: from 17 billion yen to 20.3 billion yen for the impact of *Shinsengumi!* on Kyoto, and from 23.4 billion yen to 56.5 billion yen for the impact of *Ryōma-den* on Kōchi. These revisions indicate the considerable margin for error in the forecasts; furthermore, as will be discussed in detail later, there are many methodological difficulties involved in making such estimates. Nevertheless, the forecasts have the credibility of being made by Japan's central bank, and constitute the broadly accepted 'best guestimate' for the economic impact of Taiga dramas. The figures consistently suggest an annual economic impact in the range of hundreds of millions of US dollars (Table 1).

Yet Taiga drama booms typically last for one year only. Many sites of drama-induced tourism find their visitor numbers falling back to something approaching 'normal' levels in the year following the drama (Diamond Online 2010),

Table 1 Bank of Japan forecasts of the economic impact of Taiga dramas, 2003–2011

No.	Title	Year	Average ratings	Forecast (bn yen)	Revised forecast	Prefectures
50	*Gō: himetachi no sengoku*	2011		16.2		Saga
49	*Ryōma-den*	2010	18.7%	44.4 (23.4 + 21.0)	74.5 (53.5 + 21.0)	Kōchi, Nagasaki
48	*Tenchijin*	2009	21.2%	20.4		Niigata
47	*Atsuhime*	2008	24.5%	36.4		Kagoshima
46	*Fūrin kazan*	2007	18.7%	10.9		Nagano
45	*Kōmyō ga tsuji*	2006	20.9%	13.5		Kōchi
44	*Yoshitsune*	2005	19.5%	17.9		Yamaguchi
43	*Shinsengumi!*	2004	17.4%	17.0	20.3	Kyoto
42	*Musashi*	2003	16.7%	14.8		Yamaguchi

Sources: Ratings from Video Data Research (2012); Impacts from Bank of Japan (2011); Diamond Online (2010).

Note: Billion yen = thousand million (ten *oku*) yen = approximately 10 million USD (at 100 yen to the dollar).

although some of the sites discussed in this article have seen their base-level tourist numbers ratcheted up as a result of the drama. Overall, drama-induced tourism is effectively defined as additional tourist activity to sites linked with the drama that occurs in the calendar year that the drama is broadcast.

Tourism induced by *Shinsengumi!* (2004) and *Ryōma-den* (2010)

In order to explore further the dynamics of drama-induced tourism, this article examines the tourism generated by two dramas set in the Bakumatsu period (1853–1868): *Shinsengumi!* and *Ryōma-den*. Both featured men who are among the most revered heroes of the era: Hijikata Toshizō[2] and Sakamoto Ryōma. These two men are frequently paired as iconic representatives of the pro-bakufu and pro-restoration camps. Both died around the time of the restoration (Sakamoto in 1867 and Hijikata in 1869).

This article looks at three important sites of drama-induced tourism for both dramas. The first is Hakodate in Hokkaido. Hijikata and Sakamoto may have been sworn enemies in life, but both have achieved 'local hero' status in death in Hakodate, where there are museums chronicling their lives and deeds. The second is their birthplaces, where their local hero status is arguably strongest. For Hijikata this is Hino city in western Tokyo; for Sakamoto it is Kōchi in Shikoku. Finally, the article looks at Kyoto, where both men played such important roles in the turbulent decade of the 1860s. Analysis of these four sites reveals the variety of ways in which localities benefit from drama-induced tourism.

Hakodate 2004: the Shinsengumi! boom

Hakodate is a city of about 280,000 people at the southern tip of Hokkaido. It is a popular tourist destination with around five million visitors a year entering its

JAPANESE POPULAR CULTURE AND CONTENTS TOURISM

various attractions (see Figure 2 below). The night view from Mt Hakodate of the city on a peninsula jutting out into the Tsugaru Straits is rated as one of the world's three best night views alongside Hong Kong and Naples (JNTO 2013). As in many other Japanese tourist destinations, hot springs and local cuisine are also attractions. But Bakumatsu history plays a crucial role in the city's history and identity. Following the Treaty of Peace and Amity signed between Japan and the US in 1854, Hakodate port was partially opened for provisioning foreign ships, and it was opened completely as one of the treaty ports in 1859. The Motomachi area of the city at the foot of Mt Hakodate has many buildings and churches from this period, such as the former British consulate, now a teahouse.

Recognizing the strategic importance of the port and Ezo (from 1869 called Hokkaido), the Tokugawa bakufu built Goryōkaku Fort (constructed 1857–1866), a pentagonal fort in a European design. Goryōkaku Fort was the site of the last stand of Tokugawa loyalists led by Enomoto Takeaki during the last battle of the Boshin War, the Battle of Hakodate, which culminated in May 1869.

Hijikata Toshizō was one of the Tokugawa loyalists who fought under Enomoto in Hakodate. He became vice-commander of the Shinsengumi, a shogunal guard unit formed in 1863 to accompany shogun Tokugawa Iemochi on his visit from Edo to the imperial capital Kyoto. In the 1860s, the Shinsengumi gained a fearsome reputation for their assassination of imperial loyalists in Kyoto. Kondō took control of the Shinsengumi, originally led by Kondō Isami and Serizawa Kamo, after assassinating Serizawa. Hijikata became Kondō's right-hand man, and, following Kondō's capture and execution in May 1868, became *de facto* leader of the Shinsengumi. He joined Enomoto's force in Sendai *en route* to Hakodate in the autumn of 1868. Hijikata died on 11 May 1869 while riding to relieve his Shinsengumi comrades besieged in the Motomachi area during the Battle of Hakodate (Hillsborough 2005).

Dispassionate examinations of Hijikata's exploits in the Shinsengumi do not immediately suggest hero status. As their vice-commander, he earned the nickname '*oni no fukuchō*' (demon vice-commander) and was notorious for the strictness with which he enforced Shinsengumi rules, including death by seppuku for those who transgressed. He was renowned as a ruthless killer, torturer and womanizer. Nevertheless, he embodies the most precious of samurai virtues: self-sacrifice and loyalty to the bitter end. The most famous image of Hijikata (Figure 1) has undoubtedly contributed to his posthumous hero status, too. He is arguably *the* poster boy of Bakumatsu history, leading Kohinata Eri (a leading *rekijo*, 'female history fan' author – see the article by Sugawa-Shimada Akiko in this issue) to comment: 'When asked who is the number one *ikemen* [hunk] of the bakumatsu period, many people will probably say Hijikata Toshizō. He was true to bushido to the end, and is drop dead gorgeous' (Kohinata 2010, p. 190).

Figure 1 Hijikata Toshizō

Hijikata has long been a local hero in Hakodate. His exploits feature prominently in the exhibits in Goryōkaku Tower that overlooks the fort. It is Hijikata's
face, more than any other, that adorns the souvenirs on sale in the tower shop.
During the Goryōkaku Festival, held since 1970 on the third weekend in May,
there is even a competition to re-enact his death (2014 saw the twenty-seventh
contest). In 2003, a private museum (Hijikata Takuboku Museum)[3] about his
life and deeds was opened. And in the inaugural 'mock election' of historical figures held on 10 January 2011 by Hakodate city during the municipal coming of
age ceremony (*seijinshiki*), an event designed to encourage new adults to exercise
their suffrage, Hijikata topped the vote with sixty-eight out of 143 votes (only 9
per cent of ceremony attendees voted). Sakamoto Ryōma came second with
forty, poet Ishikawa Takuboku came third with twenty-two, and Edo-period
merchant Takadaya Kahee came fourth with ten (*Hokkaidō shinbun* 2011a).

When Hijikata and the Shinsengumi took leading roles in NHK's Taiga drama
in 2004, therefore, Hakodate was a prime candidate for a drama-induced tourism
boom. *Shinsengumi!*'s average viewing ratings of 17.4 per cent (over forty-nine
episodes broadcast 11 January 2004 to 12 December) were not particularly

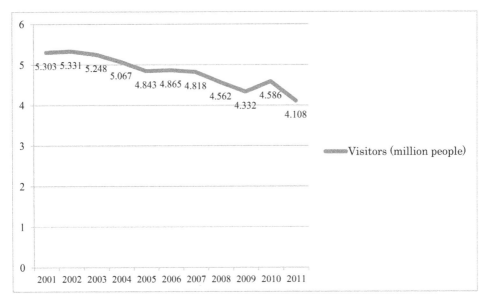

Figure 2 Total visitors to Hakodate's tourist sites, 2001–2011 (Hakodate City 2012)

strong compared to other Taiga dramas. Nevertheless, on 3 April, the *Hokkaidō shinbun* reported:

> In the midst of the nationwide Shinsengumi boom caused by NHK's Taiga Drama *Shinsengumi!*, many tourists are visiting Hakodate, where Shinsengumi vice-commander Hijikata Toshizō spent his final days. They are attracted by his and the Shinsengumi's loyalty in fighting to the bitter end for the bakufu. The effect of the drama on tourist numbers is expected to be in the tens of thousands, and sales of related merchandise are brisk.
>
> (Hokkaidō shinbun 2004a)

Seven months later in November, the talk was still of a boom. However, *Hokkaidō shinbun* changed the word 'boom' (*būmu*) to 'special procurement' (*tokuju*) in its headline. This revealing change indicated that, while merchandise sales were going well, tourist numbers were a problem: the gift shop at Goryōkaku Tower reported a 70 per cent increase in sales of Shinsengumi goods in comparison to the previous year, but was reported as saying the boom had only applied the brakes to declining visitor numbers (*Hokkaidō shinbun* 2004b). Figure 2 shows this longer-term decline in visitor numbers to Hakodate that *Shinsengumi!* could not reverse.

These aggregate data for the whole city are reflected in visitor numbers to Goryōkaku Tower, an essential site for any tourists in Hakodate primarily on the trail of Shinsengumi history. In the data in Figure 3 the middle bar for each month represents visitor numbers during 2004 when *Shinsengumi!* was broadcast. The

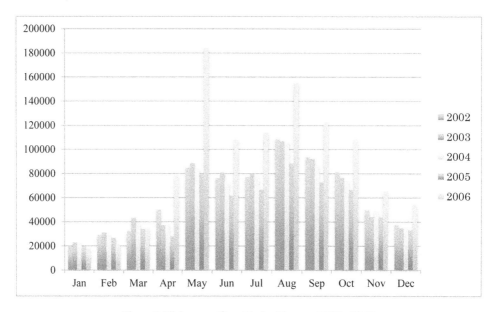

Figure 3 Visitors to Goryōkaku Tower, 2002–2006

most common trend (in nine months out of twelve, namely all months bar April, November and December) is for a drop in visitor numbers in 2004 compared to the figures for the previous year, followed by another drop in the corresponding month the following year.

Such data, however, do not disprove the existence of the Shinsengumi boom. On 21 November 2004, *Hokkaidō shinbun* (2004b) reported that the number of visitors to the Hijikata museum[4] was 60,000, or double the numbers in the same period the previous year. People who visited Hakodate on a pilgrimage to Shinsengumi sites would most likely visit both the Hijikata museum and Goryōkaku Tower. A boom of 30,000 to 40,000 extra drama-induced tourists to both sites, therefore, would be a reasonable estimate. An average of about 3,000 extra visitors a month at Goryōkaku Tower would be enough to act as a brake on the decline without reversing the downward trend in visitor numbers.

The city's annual report on tourism for the financial year 2004 (Hakodate City 2005) cites two reasons for longer-term decline: natural disasters and increased foreign travel. The year 2004 was a particularly devastating typhoon season, especially in Hokkaido, which is usually spared the brunt of typhoons. Typhoon number 18 in September caused considerable damage within Hokkaido and disrupted the late summer travel season. Then in October there was the devastating Chuetsu earthquake that hit Niigata prefecture. While not directly affecting Hokkaido, this earthquake precipitated an overall slowdown in tourist activity, through either 'restraint' (*jishuku*) following the earthquake or economic knock-on effects. The second reason for the drop in tourist numbers to Hakodate was increased foreign travel. According to the report, this was primarily a result of the Olympics held in Athens and increased travel to South Korea at the peak of the *Winter sonata* boom. In other words, one drama-induced tourism boom was trumping another.

There is one other factor to be considered. The series broadcast in 2004 had focused on Shinsengumi commander, Kondō Isami, rather than Hijikata. As an encore, and in response to popular demand (Hijikata has many more fans than Kondō), a New Year's Taiga Drama Special titled *Shinsengumi! The last days of Hijikata Toshizō* was broadcast in January 2006. This covered the Battle of Hakodate and Hijikata's death, which had been omitted from the 2004 series (Lee 2011, pp. 173–174). This drama would arguably have been a much more direct inducer of tourism to Hakodate because it focused on Hijikata's final days in Hakodate. But, as can be seen in Figure 3, this telefilm did not induce any noticeable rise in tourists. January is in the depths of winter and the tourism off-season. More significantly, the new Goryōkaku Tower was just about to be opened that April. Many people had waited to visit this new site, which was considerably taller than the old tower and contained new exhibits. As can be seen in Figure 3, there was a massive spike in visitors from April 2006.

Overall, the early estimates coming from the Hakodate Tourism Bureau of a *Shinsengumi!* boom amounting to 'tens of thousands' of extra visitors was close to the mark (*Hokkaidō shinbun* 2004a). In the context of the total tourism sector of around five million tourists a year, the Shinsengumi boom (including knock-on effects, such as visits to other sites like Mt Hakodate's night view by *Shinsengumi!* fans) amounted to perhaps a few percentage points of the Hakodate tourist industry for that year at most. So, while local media initially reported with enthusiasm evidence of the boom and provided anecdotal evidence such as 'many more visitors' or 'brisk sales of merchandise', toward the end of the year the failure to arrest an overall decline in visitor numbers was the main story. Rather than a decisive event in the tourism calendar for 2004, the boom was a bonus for Shinsengumi-related sites in the midst of difficult times for the tourism sector as a whole.

Hakodate 2010: the Ryōma-den boom

Hakodate is not the first place that most people would think to look for evidence of a tourism boom induced by a drama about the life of Sakamoto Ryōma (Figure 4). From the domain of Tosa (present-day Kōchi prefecture) in Shikoku, Sakamoto is one of Japan's most popular historical figures. Among his numerous achievements are the brokering of the Satsuma–Chōshū Alliance in 1866 (that paved the way for the two domains to finally topple the Tokugawa bakufu), the establishment of Japan's first trading company (Kaientai) and writing the blueprints for the Meiji State (the Senchū Hassaku, literally 'Eight Policies

Figure 4 Sakamoto Ryōma

Composed on a Ship'). Sakamoto was assassinated in Kyoto in 1867, just before the Meiji Restoration. He never set foot in Ezo.

However, in 2010 the broadcast of *Ryōma-den* coincided with three happenings: the strongest growth in tourist numbers in Hakodate in a decade (see Figure 2), the largest economic effect of any Taiga drama in recent times (see Table 1) and the first full year of operation of the Hokkaido Sakamoto Ryōma Museum. Were there any significant links between these happenings?

But first, how and why was Sakamoto adopted as a local Hakodate hero? Sakamoto may have never been to Ezo in his lifetime, but he passionately advocated the colonization of Ezo, which would become Meiji government policy after his death. References in letters suggest that Ryōma's wife Oryō was learning the Ainu language in preparation for Sakamoto's plans to extend the reach of his Kaientai trading company to Ezo. The Hokkaido connection then continued after Sakamoto's death when his nephew, Sakamoto Naohiro, settled in the Kitami area in northern Hokkaido in 1897 (Haraguchi 2010, pp. 10–28, 45). Naohiro's grandson, Naoyuki, became a revered Hokkaido landscape painter, and his work is displayed in the Hokkaido Sakamoto Ryōma Museum.

These connections were all significant, but ultimately Sakamoto's enduring popularity as a visionary of the bakumatsu period was the real driving force behind the museum. The museum's establishment, as with the Hijikata museum, reflects the enduring popularity of historical contents and their usefulness as tourism resources.

The museum had been at the planning stage since 2002, so it was fortuitous for the NPO (non-profit organisation) behind the project that so soon after the official opening they could ride the wave of the *Ryōma-den* boom.[5] *Hokkaidō shinbun* (2010) reported that with 'a Taiga Drama tail wind', visitors were coming from all over Japan to the new museum. There were 3,000 visitors in the first month after the official opening, many of whom were *rekijo* (female history fans). Ultimately, the museum had 75,000 visitors in its first fifteen months of operation to February 2011 (Museum Staff, interview 6 March 2011). The city's tourism report (Hakodate City 2011a) also mentions the opening of a reconstruction of the bakumatsu period Hakodate Magistrate's Office in Goryōkaku Fort and the reopening of the Hakodate Race Course as the main reasons for the rise in tourist numbers to Hakodate's sites. In 2010, 'popular new sites' was the key phrase in Hakodate, just as it had been in 2006, when the opening of the new Goryōkaku Tower helped Hakodate achieve the only other increase in overall tourist numbers during the decade.

In sum, visitor numbers to the Hokkaido Sakamoto Ryōma Museum were undoubtedly boosted by NHK's drama. They also compare favourably to visitor figures at the Hijikata Takuboku Museum during the 2004 *Shinsengumi!* boom (perhaps also a function of its convenient location downtown compared to the slightly out-of-the-way location of the Hijikata museum). Ultimately, without reliable series data – the museum opened in November 2009, only a month and a half before *Ryōma-den* began, and then on 11 March 2011 the triple disaster caused a 24 per cent drop in tourist numbers in Hakodate from April to July (Hakodate City 2011b, p. 1) – we cannot ascertain the precise extent of the drama-induced tourism boom in Hakodate. The evidence remains anecdotal.

Kōchi 2010: the Ryōma-den boom

There is no such problem of a lack of series data in Sakamoto's home prefecture of Kōchi, however, and neither is there much ambiguity over the colossal impact of the drama on levels of tourism. Figure 5 shows that the number of visitors to four of the key sites in Kōchi related to Sakamoto tripled in the year that the drama was shown. Furthermore, the figures do not include the 924,903 people who visited the Ryōma Expo (Tosa Ryōma Deai Haku)[6] during its 360 days from January 2010 to January 2011 (*Kōchi shinbun* 2011). Kōchi Ryōma Roman Shachū (an exhibit next to Kōchi Station) was the main attraction with 616,416 visitors in 2010.

According to Bank of Japan calculations, the total economic impact of the *Ryōma-den* boom on Kōchi was 53.5 billion yen, or 2.4 per cent of prefectural

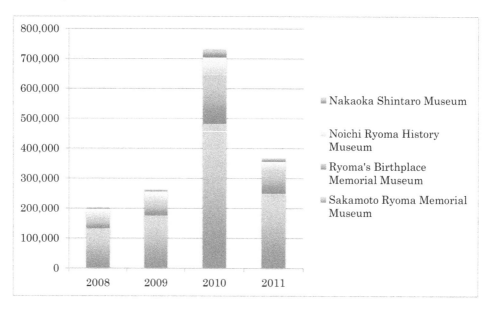

Figure 5 Visitors to four sites related to Sakamoto Ryoma in Kōchi, 2008–2011, compiled from various Kōchi Government Annual Reports, available from http://www.pref.kochi.lg.jp/soshiki/020101/20doutai.html [Accessed 30 April 2012].

GDP (Bank of Japan 2011). This more than doubled the estimates prior to the drama of 23.4 billion yen (Bank of Japan 2009a), which, when combined with the estimates for Nagasaki (where Sakamoto's Kaientai operations were based) of 21 billion yen (Bank of Japan 2009b) made the initial estimate of 44.4 billion yen (see Table 1). These Bank of Japan reports outline the methodology by which the figures are attained: (estimated) increases in tourist numbers are multiplied by average expenditure for day visitors and overnight visitors, and then other effects (such as the impact of the national economic stimulus package making expressway tolls a flat 1,000 yen charge on weekends in 2010) are factored out. With so many variables and assumptions in the calculation (such as which year is deemed to be the base year against which increases in tourism are measured), the guestimate nature of the figure becomes apparent.

Of more relevance here than the precise monetary value of the boom are some of the local conditions that made the *Ryōma-den* boom so marked in Kōchi, despite average viewing figures at the lower end of the range for Taiga dramas (18.7 per cent).

First is simply Sakamoto's popularity, in other words, the quality of the historical contents. Sakamoto is arguably the most popular historical figure in Japan and indisputably Kōchi's most famous son: the regional airport, Kōchi Ryōma Airport, is even named after him. His life story has all the ingredients of an epic drama: adventure (leaving Tosa to seek his destiny in Edo), romance (his marriage to Oryō and the 'first honeymoon' in Japan), innovation (setting up the first trading company), political vision (negotiating the Satsuma-Chōshū Alliance) and tragedy (his assassination before his visions of a new Japan could be realized). Unlike many of his contemporary *shishi* (men of high principles) in the anti-Tokugawa camp, his reputation is largely unsullied by the political killings of the 1860s, although he did plan to assassinate Katsu Kaishū until Katsu persuaded Sakamoto to join him as his *deshi* (apprentice) and strengthen the Japanese navy instead. Overall, Sakamoto's reputation is of vision not violence, which makes him a role model to this day. As with many historical figures, however, his contemporary image is based on considerable myth-making, and Fukuyama Masaharu, the actor who played Sakamoto, 'hit the nail on the head when he said that Sakamoto Ryōma is the kind of person onto whom anyone can project themselves' (Corkhill 2009). In short, the appealing and malleable quality of the contents (Sakamoto's life story) was a key element of the boom.

Second is the clearly defined destination for *Ryōma-den* fans. There are other localities that benefited from the *Ryōma-den* boom, such as Kyoto, Nagasaki and, to a lesser extent, Hakodate. But, for fans on a tourist pilgrimage to sites relating to Sakamoto, Kōchi is the place to go. With a range of established sites (the four museums in Figure 5, the statue of Sakamoto at Katsurahama beach and Kōchi Castle) as well as special events (Ryōma Expo) and other minor sites (such as the path Sakamoto took when he left Tosa in 1862), there was a clear itinerary of heritage tourist sites for fans to visit.

Third, the number/range of sites and the location of Kōchi on the southern coast of Shikoku would generate a proportionately large number of overnight visitors. Kōchi is the sort of distance from many major population centres on Honshu (stretching from Kyoto to Hiroshima) to make it a viable overnight trip but not a day trip. Adding accommodation and food to the tourist expenditure equation quickly multiplies the economic benefits to a locality in comparison to sites where day-trippers predominate.

Fourth, the number of visitors was boosted by a policy in operation in 2010 that capped expressway tolls at 1,000 yen on weekends and on holidays. The fact that the Bank of Japan tried to filter out this impact in its calculations, and also the mentions of the policy in a Kōchi government report (2010) about the additional traffic measures laid on for tourists at Katsurahama Beach (parking and shuttle buses), indicate that the *Ryōma-den* boom in Kōchi was greatly amplified by this policy.

For a variety of reasons, therefore, *Ryōma-den* induced huge levels of tourism in Kōchi during 2010. Additional visitors to Sakamoto-related museums (there were about 470,000 more visitors than in 2009 to the museums in Figure 5) and the Ryōma Expo held to coincide with the drama (a total of 924,903 visitors) numbered about 1.4 million. Many of these visitors were on overnight trips, which multiplied the economic effects through higher spending on food and accommodation. On the available evidence, *Ryōma-den* precipitated the biggest tourism boom of any Taiga drama to date.

Hino 2004: the Shinsengumi! boom

The critical role of factors other than the drama itself — such as the existing tourist infrastructure and policies favourable to tourism creation — are clarified further when the *Ryōma-den* boom in Kōchi is contrasted with the *Shinsengumi!* boom in Hino. Hino city is in western Tokyo in the midst of the sprawling metropolis that stretches from Chiba in the east to Yokohama in the west. Hino is the birthplace of a number of Shinsengumi members, including Hijikata. The name of its flagship tourist site, *Shinsengumi no furusato rekishikan* (Home of the Shinsengumi Historical Museum), epitomizes the city's claim to be the authentic site for Shinsengumi-related tourism.

This authenticity is greatly enhanced by the direct participation of descendants or relatives of Shinsengumi members in the contemporary sites. The museums in Hino to Hijikata, Inoue Genzaburō and Satō Hikogoro are all spaces in the private residences of those families. The large number of houses in the proximity of the Hijikata Toshizō museum that have the surname Hijikata on the front gate indicates how that area of Hino has been passed down from generation to generation by the Hijikata clan. They and other Shinsengumi descendants almost have the status of local aristocracy, and the family-run museums comprise primarily displays of family heirlooms. The traditions of the Tennen Rishin fencing school (in which many Shinsengumi members were trained) are carried on to this day, and a publicity pamphlet for the fencing school (picked up in March 2011) had a photo of Inoue Masao (a descendant of Genzaburō) facing off with Miyagawa Seizō, a fifth-generation descendant of Kondo Isami. In terms of tourism creation and economic terms, however, the three family museums have a minimal impact. They open only a few days a month and entry is for a nominal fee. These are sites to pass down family memories of Shinsengumi members rather than commercial enterprises running on a financial profit basis.

In other respects, too, Hino city was not particularly suited to cashing in on the *Shinsengumi!* boom in 2004. As a suburban area in the Tokyo megalopolis, Hino is not a place to which people will make overnight trips, and therefore the impacts of the tourism boom were dissipated over a much wider area within Tokyo. Nor is it a place that people will visit unless they are specifically interested in Shinsengumi sites (the other major tourist site in the city is Tama Zoological Park). There is little opportunistic drama-induced tourism (see the introduction to this special edition), meaning that people visit Hino primarily for other reasons but then decide on a whim to include Shinsengumi sites on the itinerary. Many key sites are free, such as the statue of Hijikata at Takahata Fudoson Temple; and the Home of the Shinsengumi museum opened only in 2005, the year *after* NHK's drama. The typical drama-induced tourist in Hino was most probably a day-tripper who had the whole Shinsengumi experience in Hino for a few thousand yen in entrance fees plus lunch and souvenirs before returning home or to a hotel elsewhere. The location and characteristics of

Hino as a city, therefore, meant that there was a low financial return for such prime historical assets.

This is not to say that the city did not try to exploit the increased interest in the Shinsengumi precipitated by NHK's drama. The city ran a Shinsengumi Festa throughout 2004 that attracted a total of 293,878 visitors. One-day Shinsengumi tours were taken by over 500 people and more than 1,600 people participated in walking tours of the sites (unpublished Hino City documents). There is other anecdotal evidence of the Shinsengumi boom in 2004, such as the approximately 30 per cent increase in visitors at the Hijikata Toshizō museum and the hour-long waits outside before visitors could enter the museum (Hijikata Yoko, interview 3 March 2011).

Overall, however, there is little evidence of the multi-billion yen booms that have been witnessed in other locations of Taiga dramas. The Bank of Japan did not even attempt a survey of the impact on Hino, even though it was the 'Home of the Shinsengumi'. Indeed, visitor numbers to the Home of the Shinsengumi museum indicate just how little economic effect the Bank of Japan would have found: with about 10,000 visitors a year since 2005 and adults paying only 200 yen to enter the museum, the annual revenue through entrance fees equates to less than the annual salary of one member of staff. Hino city heavily subsidizes the preservation of the city's heritage. There is also an annual Shinsengumi festival on the second weekend in May (the closest date to Hijikata's death and a week before the Goryōkaku Festival in Hakodate), but this too is heavily subsidized by local people as either participants or taxpayers. Total visitor numbers to Hino in 2004 (around 300,000) were also small in comparison to visitors to Ryōma sites in Kōchi in 2010. The Shinsengumi Festa attracted only one third of the people attracted by the Ryōma Expo, despite being an easy day-trip distance from the tens of millions of people in the Tokyo megalopolis, and in Kōchi there was museum visitation on top of the Ryōma Expo figures. So, while there was clearly a large amount of interested generated in Shinsengumi sites by NHK's drama, Hino as a city simply was not able to convert that into a significant economic effect.

Kyoto 2004 and 2010: the Shinsengumi! and Ryōma-den booms

The final location for this study of tourism induced by the two dramas is Kyoto, where Shinsengumi and Imperial loyalists battled it out on the streets in the mid-1860s, and where Sakamoto was assassinated in 1867.

When the Bank of Japan carried out its economic forecast of the impact of drama-induced tourism on Kyoto in 2004, it estimated that a million extra visitors to Kyoto would have an economic impact of 17 billion yen, of which 2.2 billion would be spent on transportation, 10.5 billion on accommodation and food and 3.7 billion on merchandise. The significance of these figures went beyond

97

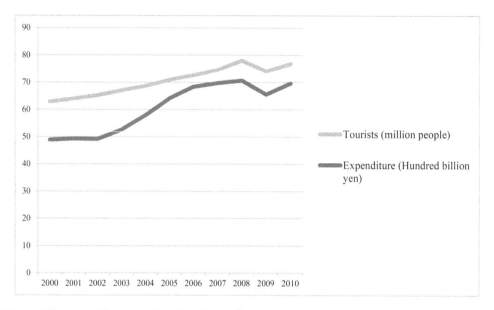

Figure 6 Visitors to Kyoto and Tourism Expenditure, 2000-2010. Source: Kyoto City Government 2011 (Kyoto City Government 2011). Hundred billion yen = one hundred thousand million (thousand *oku*) yen = approximately 1 billion USD (at 100 yen to the dollar).

simple estimates: they were key evidence used for a 2005 government report that asserted the potential of contents tourism (Ministry of Land, Infrastructure, Transport and Tourism *et al.* 2005, p. 52). Furthermore, the scale of the boom caused the estimates to be raised to 20.3 billion yen after the series had finished.

There is no equivalent survey for the effects of the *Ryōma-den* boom in Kyoto. However, the key issue in the case of assessing drama-induced tourism in Kyoto is separating out drama-induced tourism from other forms of tourism in the historical and cultural capital of Japan. Figure 6 shows total tourist numbers and the economic impact of tourism in Kyoto in the 2000s.

The aggregate data show that any effects of drama-induced tourism are hidden in the broader picture of Kyoto's massive tourism sector. In this sense, Kyoto is similar to Hakodate: aggregate figures are of little use in assessing the impact of the drama. The Kyoto data reveal another significant complicating factor in the case of *Ryōma-den*. The year 2010 was when the tourism sector bounced back from the full effects of the 2008 global financial crisis. As in Hakodate, it is the macro-trends that really matter for major tourism cities such as Kyoto.

However, there is considerable evidence of the *Shinsengumi!* and *Ryōma-den* booms at individual sites in Kyoto. Mibudera Temple is where the Shinsengumi was formed in 1863. The grounds today contain the graves of a number of members, including Serizawa Kamo, assassinated in an internal power struggle, and the three members killed during the Ikedaya incident of 1864. Detailed records of visitor numbers are not kept, but staff I spoke to recalled busloads of tourists coming in during 2004 before visitor numbers returned to 'normal' levels after the drama finished.

There are more specific data available at the nearby Yagi Residence, which is where Serizawa was assassinated. This old house is remarkable only for the violent events that occurred within its walls and the sword damage to pillars caused during the incident remain to this day. Up until the late 1990s, the Yagi Residence received twenty to forty visitors a day. During the 2004 *Shinsengumi!* boom, there were 600 to 800 visitors, rising to 1,000 on very busy days. After the drama, visitor numbers tailed off to 100 to 200. But, when repeats of *Shinsengumi!* or other related dramas are aired, these numbers rise to 300 or 400 (interview with the tour guide, 20 May 2012). These figures indicate how some tourist sites benefit in the long term by becoming better known and more established on heritage tourism itineraries. *Shinsengumi!* ratcheted up standard visitor levels by three to four times.

It is a similar story at the Ryozen Museum of History, a museum that focuses on the bakumatsu period and features Hijikata and Sakamoto prominently, most notably in the photo area, where visitors may dress up as a Shinsengumi soldier and have their picture taken in between cardboard cut-outs of the two men. Visitor numbers to the museum are given in Figure 7.

There are unmistakable peaks in 2004 and 2010 preceded by 'lead-in booms' in 2003 and 2009 in anticipation of the dramas. It is too early to see the long-term increase in visitor numbers precipitated by *Ryōma-den*, but after *Shinsengumi!* the base level of visitors in subsequent years had increased by about 20,000

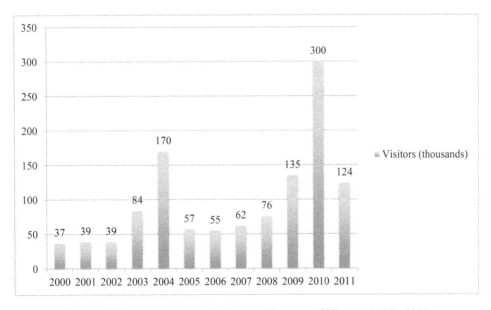

Figure 7 Visitor numbers to the Ryozen Museum of History, 2000–2011

people. Furthermore, the museum put on special exhibitions about both dramas that attracted even more visitors than the regular museum exhibits (206,000 people to a Shinsengumi exhibition in 2004 and 351,000 to a Sakamoto exhibition that ran from January 2010 for thirteen months). For a decade, the NHK Taiga drama has clearly been the single most important influence on this museum's visitor figures.

In this context, the lack of a boom in 2008, when *Atsuhime* was broadcast, is notable. There was no special exhibition, which in retrospect seems probably to have been costly, although Atsuhime's connection to Kyoto was tenuous (originally from Satsuma, she married the thirteenth shogun Tokugawa Iesada in 1856 and her life was mainly in Satsuma and Edo). However, when I visited the museum again in May 2013 there was a special exhibition about Niijima Yae to take advantage of *Yae no Sakura*. Niijima was in Aizu during the bakumatsu period, but there is a Kyoto connection in that her husband Niijima Jo set up Doshisha University in the city.

Conclusions

These investigations into drama-induced tourism in 2004 and 2010 in Hakodate, Kōchi/Hino and Kyoto suggest various conclusions.

Taiga drama-induced tourism is one of the most significant examples in the world of film-induced tourism and contents tourism. Recognition of the phenomenon over the past decade has resulted in large sets of data being produced on an annual basis. This includes the Bank of Japan forecasts, prefectural/municipal tourism reports, media reportage and academic research. In the field of film-induced tourism, where so many case studies are 'one-offs', Taiga dramas offer a rare opportunity for systematic, on-going research into contents tourism.

Taiga dramas boost existing heritage/cultural tourism rather than creating new sites for tourism. The multi-use and recycling of contents means that popular historical narratives and figures are lucrative, sustainable tourist resources, particularly in areas where a large percentage of visitors will make overnight stays rather than day trips.

There is little direct correlation between viewing figures and the amount of tourism induced. This suggests that factors other than solely the contents are key drivers of or constraints on contents tourism. Examples include the positive effects of economic stimulus measures (expressway toll reductions) and negative effects of natural disasters on the tourism sector. Film-induced tourism cannot be separated from the macro-trends in the broader tourism sector.

The state of existing tourism infrastructure and the nature of the destination massively affect the economic impact or the visibility of the impact of film-induced tourism on a locality. In large metropolises (like Tokyo) or tourist destinations with myriad tourism assets (Hakodate and Kyoto), the empirical evidence of film-induced tourism is often lost in the aggregate data or evidence exists primarily in anecdotal form. In places where drama-induced tourism has the opportunity to monopolize or dominate the tourism sector (such as Kōchi, where Sakamoto Ryōma features so prominently in the prefecture's overall identity), it shows up very clearly in local statistics. However, the effects of drama-induced tourism may be very weak, even with excellent tourism assets, if the broader destination is ill-suited to attracting tourists (such as Hino, in the Tokyo commuter belt).

In any type of destination, the quantification of film-induced tourism, whether in visitor numbers or economic impact, is virtually impossible. There are problems of measuring motivation (namely whether people visited sites as a direct result of watching the drama or not) and the economic impact (the various assumptions made in forecasting introduce large margins for error). Even so, the data for tourism induced by Taiga dramas suggests an economic impact in the hundreds of millions of dollars per year. Furthermore, as the examples of Hakodate and Hino demonstrate, there may also be significant drama-induced tourism in places where there is no systematic effort to quantify the effects of the drama. For decades NHK's Taiga dramas have been an established part of the Japanese television calendar. Now, they are undeniably an important part of the tourism calendar, too.

Notes

1. Niijima Yae actually had three nicknames corresponding to the three periods of her life: 'Bakumatsu Joan of Arc' for her role in the Boshin War, 'Handsome Woman' for her life as a Christian member of high society married to Niijima Jo (Joseph Hardy Neesima, founder of Doshisha University) and 'Japan's Nightingale' for her work in the Japanese Red Cross following her husband's death (Doshisha Women's University website: http://www.dwc.doshisha.ac.jp/yae/profile/ [Accessed 20 December 2013]). It was this first period of her life that dominated publicity for the drama, and was the projected target for the drama-induced tourism boom.
2. In *Shinsengumi!*, it was actually Kondō Isami, played by Katori Shingo, who had the leading role, not Hijikata. This was a notable change from many other dramas which tell the story from Hijikata's perspective (see Lee 2011). In the tourist sites that benefited from the *Shinsengumi!* boom, particularly in Hakodate and Hino, Hijikata is clearly the main figure. Hence, this article focuses on Hijikata.
3. As indicated by the museum's name, Hijikata Takuboku Museum (official website: http://www.romankan.com/), the museum is not only about Hijikata. It originally commemorated the poet Ishikawa Takuboku (1886–1912), who spent a brief period living in Hakodate, and whose grave is at the foot of Mt. Hakodate. The museum was opened in 1999 by Satō Yutaka, manager of a local seafood company, near the Takuboku Park on the coastal road to Hakodate airport. It attracted about 10,000 visitors a year. Many visitors said they wanted to know more about Hijikata, so Satō expanded the museum. The new Hijikata exhibits opened in 2003, a year before the *Shinsengumi!* drama (*Hokkaidō Shinbun* 2003). The museum rode the wave of the Shinsengumi! boom in 2004 and the exhibits were upgraded in 2005. At the Hijikata Takuboku Museum in 2012, the Hijikata exhibits occupy the ground floor, and the Takuboku exhibits the first floor.

4. I visited this museum on 6 March 2011 and asked for attendance data, but the museum declined to give detailed figures.

5. The first public meeting to plan the Hokkaido Sakamoto Ryōma Museum (official website: http://www.ryoma1115.com/) was on 20 January 2002 and the group was formed into an NPO that November. Initially, the aim was to open a museum in Sapporo, where the descendants of Ryōma's nephew continue to live today. The location was eventually changed to Hakodate, which was better known as a site of bakumatsu history. The proposed museum came to national attention in July 2004, when the museum organizing committee purchased one of the only 139 authenticated letters written by Ryōma for 16.3 million yen. The Ryōma NPO continued its activities holding meetings, exhibitions and starting a *juku* (evening school) in 2007 that provided various classes. Eventually, the museum was opened ahead of schedule on 15 November 2009, Ryōma's birthday. A year later, a large bronze statue of Ryōma was unveiled on 15 November 2010 just across the road (source: materials on display in the museum foyer).

6. Pamphlet: http://www.city.kochi.kochi.jp/uploaded/attachment/5638.pdf [Accessed 12 June 2014].

References

Bank of Japan, 2009a. NHK taiga dorama 'Ryōma-den' no keizai hakyū kōka. Available from: http://www3.boj.or.jp/kochi/pdf/2110k.pdf [Accessed 12 June 2014].

Bank of Japan, 2009b. NHK taiga dorama 'Ryōma-den' no hōei ni tomonau keizai kōka shizan. Available from: http://www3.boj.or.jp/nagasaki/kouhyou/2009/kouka.pdf [Accessed 2 May 2012].

Bank of Japan, 2011. NHK taiga dorama 'Ryōma-den' no keizai hakyū kōka. Available from: http://www3.boj.or.jp/kochi/pdf/2301k.pdf [Accessed 12 June 2014].

Corkhill, E., 2009. Legendary, dirty samurai gets makeover. *The Japan Times*, 25 Dec. Available from: http://www.japantimes.co.jp/text/fd20091225r1.html [Accessed 2 May 2012].

Diamond Online, 2010. 'Ryōma-den' būmu de chihō no kankōkyaku ga gekizō! Igaina hodo ōkii taiga dorama no 'chiiki uruoshi kōka'. Available from: http://diamond.jp/articles/-/8398 [Accessed 12 June 2014].

Fukushima Minpō, 2012. 'Yae no sakura' no doramakan, kyū Aizu toshokan ni seibi, rainen 1-gatsu kaikan yotei. *Fukushima Minpō*, 2 Feb. Available from: http://www.minpo.jp/view.php?pageId=4107&blockId=9930055&newsMode=article [Accessed 10 April 2012].

Hakodate City, 2005. Heisei 16-nendo jōki, raihako kankō irikomi kyakusū suii. Available from: http://www.city.hakodate.hokkaido.jp/kankou/material/h16irikomi.pdf [Accessed 25 October 2012].

Hakodate City, 2011a. Heisei 22-nendo, raihako kankō irikomi kyakusū suii. Available from: http://www.city.hakodate.hokkaido.jp/kankou/material/h22irikomi.pdf [Accessed 25 October 2012].

Hakodate City, 2011b. Heisei 23-nendo jōki, raihako kankō irikomi kyakusū suii. Available from: http://www.city.hakodate.hokkaido.jp/kankou/material/h23fh_irikomi.pdf [Accessed 25 October 2012].

Hakodate City, 2012. Raihako kankō irikomi kyakusū no suii (Shōwa 30-nendo kara). Available from: http://www.city.hakodate.hokkaido.jp/kankou/material/h23suii.pdf [Accessed 25 October 2012].

Haraguchi, I., 2010. *Sakamoto Ryōma to Hokkaidō*. Tokyo: PHP Shinsho 704.

Hillsborough, R., 2005. *Shinsengumi: the Shogun's last samurai corps*. North Clarendon, VT: Tuttle.

Hokkaidō shinbun, 2003. 'Hito 2003' Satō Yutaka, Hijikata Toshizō Hakodate kinenkan wo kaisetsu suru. *Hokkaidō shinbun*, 5 May, p. 2.

Hokkaidō shinbun, 2004a. NHK dorama de Shinsengumi būmu. *Hokkaidō shinbun*, 3 April, p. 1.

Hokkaidō shinbun, 2004b. Shinsengumi 'tokuju' ni waita Hakodate. *Hokkaidō shinbun*, 21 Nov., p. 28.

Hokkaidō shinbun, 2010. Ryōma daisuki 'rekijo' zokuzoku. *Hokkaidō shinbun*, 6 Jan., p. 25.

Hokkaidō shinbun, 2011a. Wakamono no chie, senkyo ni. *Hokkaidō shinbun*, 5 Feb., p. 21.

Hokkaidō shinbun, 2011b. 13 nen taiga wa 'Yae no sakura'. *Hokkaidō shinbun*, 23 June, p. 30.

JNTO (Japan National Tourism Organization), 2013. Around Hakodate. Available from: http://www.jnto.go.jp/eng/location/regional/hokkaido/hakodatekougai.html [Accessed 20 Dec. 2013].

Kōchi Government, 2010. Gōruden uīku no kankō to sangyō fukkō. Available from: http://www.pref.kochi.lg.jp/chiji/h22-05.html [Accessed 20 Dec. 2013].

Kōchi shinbun, 2011. Tosa deaihaku heimaku. Shūkyaku 92-man nin Ryōma in kansha. *Kōchi shinbun*, 11 Jan. Available from http://203.139.202.230/09ryomadeai/110111ryomadeai02.htm [Accessed 30 April 2012].

Kohinata, E., 2010. *Ikemen bakumatsushi*. Tokyo: PHP Shinsho 677.

Kyoto City Government, 2011. Heisei 22-nen kenkō irekomi kyakusū oyobi kankō shōhirui ni tsuite. Available from: http://www.pref.kyoto.jp/news/kanko/1313467284813.pdf [Accessed 12 June 2014].

Lee, R. 2011. Romanticising Shinsengumi in contemporary Japan. *New Voices* 4, 168–187.

Ministry of Land, Intrastructure, Transport and Tourism, the Ministry of Economy, Trade and Industry, and the Agency for Cultural Affairs, 2005. Eizō tō kontentsu no sakusei, katsuyō ni yoru chiiki shinkō no arikata ni kansuru chōsa hōkokusho. Available from http://www.mlit.go.jp/kokudokeikaku/souhatu/h16seika/12eizou/12eizou.htm [Accessed 12 June 2014].

NHK, 2011. *NHK taiga dorama taizen, 50 sakuhin tettei gaido*. Tokyo: NHK shuppan.

Standish, I., 2005. *A new history of Japanese cinema: a century of narrative film*. New York, Continuum.

Video Data Research, 2012. Kako no shichōritsu dēta, NHK taiga dorama. Available from: http://www.videor.co.jp/data/ratedata/program/03taiga.htm [Accessed 12 June 2014].

Philip Seaton is a professor in the International Student Center, Hokkaido University, where he is the convenor of the Modern Japanese Studies Program. He is the author of *Japan's contested war memories* (Routledge, 2007) and won the Daiwa Japan Forum Prize in 2006 for the article 'Reporting the 2001 textbook and Yasukuni Shrine controversies'.

Index

Note: Page numbers in *italic* type refer to illustrations

For Product Safety Concerns and Information please contact our EU
representative GPSR@taylorandfrancis.com
Taylor & Francis Verlag GmbH, Kaufingerstraße 24, 80331 München, Germany

www.ingramcontent.com/pod-product-compliance
Ingram Content Group UK Ltd.
Pitfield, Milton Keynes, MK11 3LW, UK
UKHW011456240425
457818UK00021B/852